Leading with Passion
Simple and Creative Ways to Inspire Your Team

by
Matt Modugno

iUniverse, Inc.

New York   Bloomington

Leading with Passion
Simple and Creative Ways to Inspire Your Team

iUniverse books may be ordered through booksellers or by contacting:

iUniverse
1663 Liberty Drive
Bloomington, IN 47403
www.iuniverse.com
1-800-Authors (1-800-288-4677)

Because of the dynamic nature of the Internet, any Web addresses or links
contained in this book may have changed since publication and may no
longer be valid. The views expressed in this work are solely those of the
author and do not necessarily reflect the views of the publisher,
and the publisher hereby disclaims any responsibility for them.

ISBN: 978-0-595-49593-1 (pbk)
ISBN: 978-0-595-61165-2 (ebk)

Printed in the United States of America

Anyone inspired to write a book owes a lot to the many people who help form that inspiration. I'm no different, and I am very appreciative of those who have lit the fire in my belly and taken an interest in me at varying points in my life.

To my parents and family for showing me the value of hard work and the way to lead a decent life. Special thanks and love to Mom for having the courage to be a single parent. She is as much my friend as my parent.

To my high school basketball coach for wanting me to quit—and the joy of proving him wrong.

To Loyola Marymount University for inviting me to learn and develop my skills. The school has a big heart, and I felt lucky to be a student at this great university.

To the incredible people at First Franklin Financial who gave me a shot as a young kid, allowed me to make mistakes, and provided me with some phenomenal career opportunities. The people I met and worked with will be lifelong friends, especially those with Team Laguna and Team San Diego. The commitment, dedication, and open-mindedness from these people allowed us to reach great heights together. We proved we could work hard and be successful while still having fun doing it.

To my wife, Stacy—without your support this experience would not have been possible. Thank you for being my first editor, and thank you for your thoughts and inspirations that were included in this book ... I love you. Together, the journey keeps getting more fun!

Finally to my kids, Samantha and Luke, because no one was more excited about my writing a book. The joy and excitement in their eyes kept me wanting to continue this endeavor. And so, I want them to know that in life it doesn't matter if you win or lose: all that matters is that you gave it all you had—all your creativity, all your energy, and all your passion to be the best you could. I hope you enjoy reading the book as much as I did writing it.

Cheers!

Contents

"If your actions inspire others to dream more, learn more, do more and become more, you are a leader."

—*John Quincy Adams,*

6th U.S. President (1825–1829)

I spent eighteen years in the mortgage industry, fifteen of them leading people. I had the great fortune to be a member of a unique business team whose story needed to be told and remembered. Like any inspired author, I felt I had a unique and compelling story inside of me which was burning to get out.

The inspiration for this book, and the reason it was written, all boil down to two simple points. First, I believe my team and I reached a level very few do. It was beautiful to watch teammates of all ages, backgrounds, and socioeconomic groups who filled all positions from operations to sales peacefully coexisting while pushing each other towards excellence. Second, I believe business leadership in America needs to grow, and the leaders need to push themselves harder to think creatively to get the most out of their team. Connecting with people, inspiring, coaching, explaining change, and influencing are powerful components of productive leadership. However, all of these responsibilities fall squarely on the shoulders of the leader and depend on their abilities to effectively and genuinely communicate their thoughts and feelings. These attributes mean more than a sound business strategy or a healthy P&L. Great plans can and do fail because of inadequate leadership and poor execution.

I've managed people from eighteen years old to sixty-five, and I'll let you in on a little secret they all have in common. One, they want to be treated fairly. Two, they want to be treated with respect. Three, they want to contribute to something significant and worthwhile, and four, they want to have some fun along the way. Good leaders recognize these basic needs and fulfill them. However, leaders need to constantly evolve and re-evaluate their methods of communicating. Lazy leaders—those who resort to the style most comfortable for them—aren't leaders at all.

This book is bold in that it will challenge leaders to become better, in part by re-evaluating themselves and their leadership style. At the same time, it is meant to be a useful resource manual for leaders to keep at their desks and generate creative thoughts to inspire their teams to give their best effort. It has less leadership theory and more practical, day-to-day ideas to galvanize the connection between a leader and his or her staff. I've filled this book with useful tips and ideas that have worked in the real world as I led my team of professionals to some great achievements.

Leadership books aren't just for business people. Ultimately, I believe good leadership is a *lifestyle* that we must practice everyday. It is not only a business skill, it is a skill that will make us better parents, teachers, coaches, community leaders, and will help us in our everyday dealings with people. In business, every organization needs to do a better job of training its leaders to take a creative and genuine path in leading others. Leadership is about dedication and a work ethic that in turn earns the respect of those you are leading. However, to arrive at your desired goal together and achieve the greatest results, a key component is your ability to connect with people and communicate effectively—and that is the central theme of this book.

Reading this book is informational.
Applying what's in this book is powerful.
Enjoy!

–Matt Modugno
June 2008

.

It was easily the toughest day in my eighteen-year work career. Earlier in the day, I had laid off eighteen of our thirty-four employees at the location I managed. That was 53 percent of my staff! The average tenure of the affected employees was six years, so these were all well-trained and very dedicated people. In addition to tenure, many of these people were a big piece of the culture and spirit of the office.

This was the subprime mortgage business in late 2007 when the crisis in the industry was causing a massive exodus. The combination of softening housing values, liberal underwriting standards, and overly aggressive loan programs contributed to the mortgage meltdown. The dedicated employees weren't responsible for the erosion of lending standards, yet they were the ones to suffer the most by losing their jobs. Executives, investors, rating agencies, and regulatory bodies allowed lax standards and guidelines to fatally damage the industry.

At about this same time, I got the greatest gift a leader can receive. After the employees received the message that their jobs had been eliminated, boxed up their personal belongings, and had a short time to reflect on what just happened, they asked me to join them at our sales manager's house for a farewell get-together. They wanted a chance to express their appreciation to me for giving them opportunities and for inspiring them to become better workers; they also just wanted to say thank you. Many of them expressed they were more concerned about how I was doing after such a brutal day rather than themselves.

I reciprocated their feelings: I was grateful and appreciative to have had such a great group to lead. I was thankful to them for being tremendous workers, for embracing change at different times so the office could succeed, for being good to each other as co-workers which produced a powerful team effort, and for being willing to run through any challenge for me.

How many layoffs go this way? I would guess not many.

In many ways that afternoon was surreal. However, as I drove home that night, it hit me: I realized why our team had such a high degree of mutual respect for each other. Why we were so successful at understanding how our team's success was really interdependent between the leader and the staff. How we needed each other to move the office forward. How each person represented a spoke in the wheel, with each spoke having a specific job to do, and no spoke being more important than the other. All of this was possible because we built our office from a foundation of trust. From that point, we became unstoppable.

Over the years, my team posted some incredible achievements. In 2004, when interest rates fell to their lowest level in fifty years, our team funded over 1400 loans in a single month. That equates to sixty-three loans closed every day, which is almost eight per working hour, or two every fifteen minutes! During the peak, on average our team took loans from start to finish in fewer than twelve days. Keep in mind, this was a time when the industry standard was taking two weeks or more just to render a loan decision. Our customer service and office efficiency was truly second to none within our industry.

The banner years of 2002 through 2006 were characterized by incredible dedication. It wasn't uncommon to see employees stay at work until 10 p.m. and arrive at 7 a.m. to get a jump-start on their day. They did it out of their love for the company and their desire to deliver excellent work. The mortgage business was a robust one, and my team was performing at its highest level.

The way in which the mortgage industry was torn apart during 2006 and 2007 was disappointing; however, the tremendous company culture and team chemistry I experienced over my entire eighteen-year career was worth remembering. My story as a member of this great team is the cornerstone of this book. It was a moment in time I will always appreciate.

Chapter 1

The Backdrop

*"Life is 10 percent what happens to me
and 90 percent of how I react to it"*
—Charles R. Swindoll

I vividly remember this thought from the early winter months of 2002. With twelve years in the mortgage business under my belt, I'd accepted a promotion to run the largest office in our company, which was a one-hour commute from my home. As I traveled to the office to begin my first day, a thought hit me as quickly as a Southern California traffic jam. About fifty employees at the Laguna Hills office would be anxiously awaiting answers to the following questions:

- What type of leader would I be?
- What was important to me?
- What goals would be established both for their department and the office?
- How could their contributions plug into the office structure?
- How often could they expect feedback on their performance?

- Would the fun they'd been enjoying be continued or squashed?
- What differences would there be between me and the previous branch manager?
- What changes would there be to the office culture?

Then there was the most obvious question: could this new leader continue the same type of success the team had recently experienced?

Simply put, my *competency* and *capability* would be scrutinized.

This type of introspective reflection is an important part of creating a consistent and predictable leadership style. It's not something you want to handle on the fly because you will only confuse your team. Reflecting on what type of leader you want to aspire to be is the first step towards building a foundation. Prioritizing what's most important to you is a good first step, but realize your style will evolve, and you will make mistakes. Warren Bennis, chairman of the University of Southern California's leadership institute who is widely regarded as the dean of leadership studies, says leaders should never stop learning about themselves. In *Conversations on Leadership* he adds:

> You're going to fall on your face, you're going to learn from it, and you're going to continue that for the rest of your life … know your strengths, but know your weaknesses better. (2004, 18)

As I continued my commute, I noticed I'd been in deep thought for forty minutes and my coffee was now cold. I began realizing the magnitude of what I owed my newly inherited staff. Upon my arrival in just twenty minutes, the staff would begin to fill-in the early answers to these important questions. Anxiety began to build.

Then this thought hit me.

Just as I'd done in my twelve-year career with our loan officer customers, my ability to take complex strategies and transform them into "simple to understand" messages was going to be a powerful ingredient of leading effectively. I knew making my message simple—and even fun—would be the first step in giving my staff bite-sized chunks of information that could easily be digested. I began to gain confidence I could create "followership momentum" and get the office rolling in the right direction by starting to focus on the important topics I needed to boil down into *simple* messages.

My thoughts were off and running in the right direction!

Chapter 2

Seizing the Moment

"Even if you're on the right track,
you'll get run over if you just sit there."
—*Will Rogers*

When you're promoted into a leadership role, it is crucial your effort level rises to the occasion. You are now no longer responsible merely for yourself, but for many others. That may sound like an obvious point, but I believe many leaders don't make this fundamental mind-shift. I believe there's a real shortage of effective leaders in America today. To this point, *Fortune* magazine revealed that only ten of the ninety-nine individuals in New York University's Hall of Fame for Great Americans are business leaders. To this point, Warren Bennis adds the following in "Where Have All the Leaders Gone?":

> Dr. John Platt, a scientist at the University of Michigan, recently stated what he considers to be the ten basic dangers to world survival. Of greatest significance was the possibility of some kind of nuclear war or accident which would destroy the entire human race. The second greatest danger is the possibility of a worldwide epidemic,

famine or depression. He sees as the world's third greatest danger a general failure in *the quality of the management and leadership of our institutions.* (1989, 6)

It is critical we stop this perceived erosion of leadership skills in America. Again, our effort and commitment level must rise when we take on a leadership role within our organization.

We encounter different leaders and mentors throughout our lives. In the early days, it may be our parents or grandparents, while later it may be a coach, teacher, counselor, or boss. In all these examples, these individuals are in a position to influence, direct, and motivate us. A good leader will do all of these things, but the most important attribute is a natural by-product of all these actions. Ultimately, a leadership job done well will help us extract and realize our full potential.

As humans, most employees' initial reaction is a desire to please the leader. During the first few days of school or when trying out for a sports team, we quickly try to determine what will be expected of us in order to please our leader. The same is true in a working environment. The employees are closely watching the boss, especially during the first few weeks. During this period, the staff determines what's important, what they can get away with, what work quality is expected, and what process the boss uses to make decisions. They're also seeing whether the boss plays favorites, has a sense of humor, and allows creativity and freedom. Most importantly, they watch how the boss uses power and if that person is capable of improving and bringing success to the team.

Obviously this is a very important time for a leader to establish the boundaries for the team. I call this establishing the "corral" within which the team will need to work. The prairie can't be completely open and allow all of the horses to run free.

It becomes a crucial first step for new leaders to realize this precious moment in time and use it to establish themselves, their values, and their leadership style. It is their responsibility to communicate thoughts effectively so their team can plug in and execute the strategy. As my regional boss told me when I accepted this branch manager position, "You are no longer in the business of closing home loans—you are now in the *people* business." I never forgot those words because he was exactly right. As a leader, you do not have a second chance to make a positive first impression, so *seize it at the outset*!

Chapter 3

Building the Corral

"Nothing is particularly hard if you divide it into small jobs."
—Henry Ford

After buying a new board game, what do you do first? You open the box and look for the rules page. You then read through the rules to understand how to set up, begin, and play the game. With these rules, you can begin to strategize how to play the game and determine what's fair and unfair. Setting the ground rules to a business team is no different. A leader's first step in developing a consistent and predictable approach is to build a corral. This means developing a foundation with behavioral ground rules and communicating clear boundaries for your team to work within.

The first exercise in building the corral is to create team values. This is a list of rules and behaviors the leader is asking the team to live by. These values will apply to all employees regardless of job position or skill level. Everyone from the receptionist to the highly paid sales force and managers must be held accountable to the same team values. Consistency in who is held to the values is vital to building a fair and trustworthy environment.

As a leader, you will need to invest time to develop team values that are global enough to apply to any situation you may confront, yet specific enough to serve as a relevant message to your employees. These values should be simple and concise so they are easily digested, understood, and retained.

Some companies come up with mission and vision statements that are too complex and lengthy. They create elaborate posters that resemble the U.S. Constitution and distribute them throughout their organization. Six months later, they're wondering why their team is missing targets and not delivering results. *Answer*: their message was way too complex and confusing. They didn't make it simple for the team to understand where their individual contribution could fit in and make a difference to the team's mission. As textbook-sounding as a mission statement may be, it becomes a complete failure if it isn't executed in a way that will yield positive results. Don't fall into this trap and think more complexity is better.

Robert Goffee and Gareth Jones in "Followership: It's Personal, Too" support the idea that from a sociological and psychological perspective, followers have three basic emotional criteria that must be met to allow them to be led. The first is a feeling of significance. Leaders must show followers their contributions matter. Second, followers want to feel a sense of community. They must feel a "unity of purpose around work ... and relate to one another as human beings." (1979, 172) Finally, followers want be challenged and feel excitement. Leaders must be able to inspire and bring enthusiasm to work to realize their staff's full potential. Goffee and Jones conclude, "Followers want the leader to create feelings of significance, community, and excitement—or the deal is off." (172) These are three important areas to consider when you are "building the corral" for your team.

I studied a construction company whose leadership team did a very good job in making their company mission statement stick with their employees. It was so easy to remember that when asked, each employee could easily recite the statement. It was simple, yet meaningful to the company's overall success as the employees were very much aligned behind the message. Their work flow efficiency was the best it had ever been, errors were the lowest in company history, and profits were as high as ever reported. Bottom line: they were a winning organization.

How were they able to develop an effective mission statement?

After digging down into the way they communicated with their employees and determining to what they held each other accountable, it was powerful for them to discover they'd developed a simple message that was easily retained by all, but still sufficient to drive big-time results. The construction company's mission that every employee had engrained in their minds was:

Cheaper, Faster, Better!

Simple but when you stop and reflect on that message, you realize how the mastery of each category leads to a very healthy organization. Being *cheaper* deals with cost management, *faster* with employee efficiency and customer service, and *better* with innovation and creativity. Wow, that really says it all—but on something that could still be fit inside a fortune cookie! This provided a very clear message relevant and vital to the success of the organization that every employee could remember. The company included this message on every employee's computer screen saver along with progress dials for each category, thus sharing and updating the results. This is exactly how you generate leadership momentum.

If asked, could your employees easily recite your company's mission statement?

Another example can be seen when we look at the airlines industry. Some airlines began to keep track of the time their aircrafts' wheels spent on land. They then shared this information with their employees and created a mission statement aimed at reducing that time. They knew less time on land meant more time in the air, and thus more customers served. More customers served meant more money. Brilliant yet simple!

Once again, this was a very easy message to deliver—one that could easily be disseminated throughout the organization. More importantly, it was a message employees could easily plug into and understand how they could make a difference in "moving the needle" or minimizing the time the wheels spent on land. This message was relevant to everyone, from those in the baggage department, to the employees gathering passengers at the front gate, to flight attendants assisting passengers to their seats, to the pilot ensuring the aircraft was ready for departure. Bottom line: all employees could effect change and minimize the time the airplane's wheels spent on land.

Aligning people and their contributions behind company goals is an essential part of a leader's job. At my office, I wanted to develop a similar message that was born from a simple thought, yet would have a large impact on our overall success as a team.

As I thought about our business, I realized a lot of our success hinged on our ability to work together as a team internally. The mortgage business has your typical operations-versus-sales staff friction, but it also has many internal departments that depend on each other to create effective and reliable customer experiences. For example, an *underwriter*, who is responsible to formally approve or deny a file, depends upon a *customer service representative* to connect with the customer to move the loan forward. Secondly, the customer service rep depends upon a *document department employee* to get the loan documents to the escrow company. Finally, the team then depends upon a *loan closer* to work with the escrow and title companies to fund the loan which signifies the end of the transaction. Any internal breakdown along the way could spoil everyone's hard work and result in a poor customer experience. In other words, the home loan process is similar to a classic relay race—each person must do his or her job effectively, otherwise everyone's contribution will be spoiled.

As I thought about this interdependency, I realized our team values must be effective in addressing and minimizing internal conflicts. I needed to create core values to support a process in which the operations staff, sales staff, and internal departments could seamlessly work with one another and produce a customer experience second to none. Here are the values I created:

> **Hard Work** builds excellent customer service!
> **Mutual Respect** builds teamwork!
> **Having Fun** makes work enjoyable!

From top to bottom, everyone was held to these values, with any violation meaning a trip to my office for a discussion. To break the values down, hard work is a quality essential to any team or organization. Employees who are not fully committed create slack in the organization. The goal is to get the employees to treat their work as a career rather than merely a job. When employees view their work as their careers, there is a visible difference in how they go about their work and what they are willing to do for customers or co-workers. When you treat your work as a career, you understand the bigger picture and are willing to go the extra mile, to learn more about the nuances of the business and what makes it tick, and to do things for the health of the organization.

Second, mutual respect was vital to our success due to our department interdependency. Even when tempers were raging, it was essential to our system that people approach each other with respect and courtesy. I knew I couldn't allow infighting as that could be detrimental and lead us down a path of destruction. Mutual respect was a major theme of our office. I established this by remaining true to this team value and calling people to my office when I observed actions that violated its spirit. It didn't matter if the person was our top salesperson or a temporary employee—everyone was held accountable to the value.

Finally, the team value of *having fun* sounds like a cliché rather than anything worth mentioning or establishing as a value. The truth of the matter is that burnout is a leading cause of employee disengagement. To ensure high level efforts can be sustained over time, I had to contend with this issue and think of ways to make the work environment enjoyable.

For example, within our team, we spent some time and money making our lunchroom, which we called the "lounge," a very comfortable and casual place that looked more like what you'd find in an apartment. We painted the room in soothing colors and purchased a comfortable leather couch, chair, and throw rugs along with a large flat-panel TV that had a Nintendo Wii ready for employee challenges.

Each quarter, I e-mailed ten trivia questions to the staff and offered gift cards as prizes to those with the most correct answers. The questions covered industry knowledge and underwriting guidelines, but also included general topics such as U.S. history and entertainment. I would keep the playing cards of Trivial Pursuit, Family Feud, and other board games at my desk to keep the questions fresh. I also purchased a small "Wheel of Fortune," and after a successful month, I had employees who achieved a personal best spin it for small prizes. Thinking creatively and making the work environment fun actually increased productivity because the employees wanted to give the team more of themselves. It also did wonders for work satisfaction, which is a major driver of employee productivity.

Establishing the team's core values allows a leader to provide a stable and consistent environment. These values become the commandments you want consistently followed, and establishing them up-front allows you to refer back to them if the team veers off track. Phillip Fulmer, head coach of the University of Tennessee Volunteers football team (1998 national champions), was interviewed about the importance of establishing core values within his program:

> Establish what the core values of your organization are going to be and don't veer far from those … I think discipline is extremely important… We are never too far away from our core values. (2004, 111)

My job became monitoring and balancing our team values and ensuring all three cylinders were firing at all times. I found it interesting that any time I encountered an employee who was disgruntled or had a conflict within the team, one of these three values was amiss. I had employees who respected everyone and had fun at the office, but weren't putting in the work to hit the numbers required; hence, their work ethic was lacking. Then I had employees who had a terrific work ethic and were exceeding our goals, but were constantly having run-ins with the staff, blaming fellow teammates in the face of the customer, and approaching conflicts in ways that weren't productive or professional; hence, they lacked the value of working with mutual respect. Finally, there were those who worked hard and respected their fellow employees but brought down employee morale because they never seemed to relax or have any fun on the job. I became convinced that balancing these three values was the secret sauce in taking this team to a new level of success.

Just as in building a home, the first step is to ensure you have a strong foundation, because if you don't, everything built from that point forward will be flawed and uneven, and secondary problems will arise. Here's the board that was placed in our office for our team and customers to see. It served as a visual reminder of the importance of our team values and it was our foundation.

Team Laguna Branch Values

Mutual Respect builds teamwork!

Hard Work builds excellent customer service!

Having Fun makes work enjoyable!

Chapter 4

What's the Difference between Managing and Leading?

"Before you are a leader, success is all about growing yourself. When you become a leader, success is all about growing others."
—*Jack Welch*

My definition of leadership would sound something like this:

> The ability of an individual to influence, motivate, and enable others to contribute toward the effectiveness and success of the organization of which they are members.
> It is an attitude that influences the environment around us.

While that is a solid start in terms of understanding the meaning of leadership, we need to dig deeper to discover leadership's business application and the way leaders interact with their team. Managing and leading are distinctly two different processes that carry different duties and responsibilities. University of Southern California leadership professor Warren Bennis says he sees many institutions that are very well *managed* but very poorly *led*. He questions a leader's vision and ability to prioritize tasks: "They may excel in the ability to handle the daily routine, and yet they may never ask whether the routine should be done at all." (1989, 16)

Managing is systematic and orderly; it instills predictability in a situation and controls the environment. Managers monitor processes and policies to minimize errors. In managing, the focus is predominantly on the past, present, and short-term future. A good manager ensures the company's roadmap is being followed as closely as possible and does not allow much deviation.

On the other hand, leaders are pioneers who *create* the roadmap. **Leading** involves designing the map, setting direction, aligning people, and ensuring people are giving their maximum effort to the cause. A leader's ability to influence, motivate, and inspire can be the difference between highly executed success and complete failure. A leader's focus differs from a manager's as it is predominantly on tomorrow, next month, and the distant future. So, in summary, one can say leaders create the team's roadmap while managers ensure the roadmap is followed.

Managers and leaders also differ in the degree of risk they are willing to undertake. Managers take very little risk, and when they do, it's carefully measured. However, leaders embrace risk as they understand prudent risks are what promotes growth within their company and provides them new frontiers to explore.

Management & Leadership Compared

MANAGERS	LEADERS
Systematic & organized	Set direction & offer a vision
Process & policy-oriented	Lead change
Monitor and solve problems	Explore, inspire, work creatively
Focus: Past, today, short-term future	**Focus:** Near and distant future
Risk taking: Minimal & calculated	**Risk taking:** Embrace risk. Pioneering spirit

The distinction between managing and leading can be understood when we think about the airlines industry. When we take a routine flight, many people involved in the process take on the tasks of managing. These are the folks who are very systematic and process-oriented such as the curbside baggage clerk who validates our boarding passes and checks our IDs. Other examples include the T.S.A. security attendants and the employee controlling and solving problems at the gate. Once we board the plane, flight attendants manage the process as per FAA standards. All of these employees are very systematic as they're responsible for taking care of their piece of the overall process.

In this scenario, the leader is the pilot. This is the person responsible for setting direction and ensuring the cabin is safe for travel. The pilot focuses on the future in terms of being aware of potential weather conditions and determining possible alternative routes. The pilot is specifically trained in how to react to a multitude of different scenarios and is prepared to take necessary risks if and when necessary. Even the tools available to the pilot, such as GPS, radar, and course-setting dials, are all designed to *focus on the future*.

While there are some overlap in duties between managers and leaders, there are considerably more differences. In the airline analogy above, I know I don't want my pilot focusing on managing the plane's activities as much as I want that person to be leading the plane to a safe destination. Any person in charge of a team must recognize the difference between managing and leading and be prepared to look to the future.

Chapter 5

Meetings Aren't Enough— Mobilizing People Requires More Effort

"A life is not important except in the impact it has on other lives."
—Jackie Robinson

In the leadership fable *Death by Meeting*, author Patrick Lencioni (2004) illustrates the way leaders must prepare for and embrace the meetings they conduct. According to him, failing to design a meeting that impacts participants is like a surgeon saying, "If I didn't have to operate on people, I might actually like this job" or a professional baseball player saying, "I'd love my job if I didn't have to play in these games."

There is no worse feeling than being ten minutes into leading a meeting and realizing you have lost your group. You see the glossed-over eyes and hear the murmurs of sidebar conversations. Possibly some people are even reaching for a Blackberry to check their e-mail! If a cartoonist drew narrative balloons above your employees' heads, they might be reading, "What is he trying to tell us, and where is this meeting going?" *Ouch!*

Meetings are pretty much the main activity of leaders. It is what they are paid to do—and do well. They represent golden opportunities to set direction, review expectations, acknowledge achievements, and galvanize the team. Lencioni states, "There is simply no substitute for a good meeting—a dynamic, passionate, and focused engagement." (221)

As this responsibility should be taken seriously, leaders should prepare for meetings in the way professional football players use Monday through Saturday to get ready for a Sunday game. However, too many times I've seen a leader scribbling the meeting agenda five minutes before a meeting starts. This lack of preparation is incredibly transparent to your team. The meeting's haphazard agenda will persuade your team that the material is not that important to their success. This lack of preparation gives the employee even more reason to check that Blackberry and return a few e-mails while you speak. As Lencioni teaches us, a lack of drama is the first problem with ineffective meetings.

However, although regular meetings with an organized and well-thought out agenda definitely have a place in a leader's to-do list, they aren't the only items. Administrative tasks such as setting goals, calculating the budget, evaluating performances, and creating the company mission all have their place as well. Too many times leaders barricade themselves in their offices and focus on these mundane responsibilities instead of doing follow-up work with their team. Leaders who believe a meeting is their main source of influence power over their team are sorely mistaken. Even after a successful meeting, the leaders can't consider their weekly work to be done in terms of connecting with their team and influencing contributions, attitudes, and abilities.

Leadership is most effective when it is well balanced between the tasks that must be done (*administrative*) and the tasks that can take individuals and the company to a new level (*influence power*). Too much time spent in either category will limit the team's success. When leaders spend too much time on administrative tasks and not enough on influencing their employees, it is like someone owning a beautiful car with the best wheels, radio, and interior— but no gas! The abilities to influence, inspire, coach, mentor, and train create the gas to drive any organization forward. Therefore, as a leader, the vast majority of your time should focus on these softer skills so as to move your employees from being good contributors to great contributors. Remember as a leader, "You are in the people business!" Failure to realize and polish this aspect of running a business could prove fatal to the long-term success of your organization.

You can have the best laid-out business plan, but without a staff who can work as a team and whose members are inspired and enthusiastic about their work, you have nothing worth building. The best plans fail unless there is also a healthy work environment. It all comes together when engaged and enthusiastic employees arrive in the morning for work. When treated fairly and given a healthy and fun work environment, people will give more of themselves and realize their potential to the benefit of the leader and the company.

Balancing a Leader's Contributions

Administrative Tasks	Tasks that Inspire, Influence, and Motivate
Set goals, evaluate performance	Preach perspective & clarify big picture
Establish company vision & mission	Open the books for others to see company challenges
Conduct strategy meetings	Establish clear & realistic expectations
Align people & departments	Make yourself available
Recruit	Inspire, motivate, and connect
Obtain feedback & give follow-up	Ask for employee input
Set budget & communicate out	Discuss employee career aspirations
Oversee product development	Be approachable with open door policy
Deal with payroll & accounts payable	Delegate—encourage others to take ownership

Dale Carnegie arrived in New York City in 1912 and landed a job at a YMCA teaching public speaking to adults. He learned that public speaking skills weren't the most important things these people needed. In his book,

The Leader In You, Carnegie says he realized that people needed more training in how to get along in everyday business and social contacts. "Without mastery of that very basic human skill—the ability to talk and listen to others—members of a company, a school, or a family can't thrive for long." (1993, 31) He broadened his course to include some basic human-relations skills and Dale Carnegie & Associates, Inc. was born. His books took off and thirty million copies later the Carnegie organization has grown to train more than four hundred of the Fortune 500 firms.

So, as the company or office leader, how are you going to make sure your staff members are feeling engaged, communicating with one another effectively, peacefully co-existing and giving you their maximum effort?

Read on!

Chapter 6

Enthusiasm Makes the Difference

"Nothing great was ever achieved without enthusiasm."
—Ralph Waldo Emerson

I was recently at an upscale restaurant in Napa Valley. My friends and I had never been there before, but it came highly recommended. The food was good, but the service was horrible. Many times our glasses remained empty for long periods of time, and then we must have waited a good thirty minutes to have our credit card run to pay the bill (my number one pet peeve). The ten of us walked away agreeing we would never return.

Now as I mentioned, the food quality was very good, thus meeting the basic requirement of a good restaurant experience. I view food quality as being similar to a leader's "administrative tasks," as it is a necessary item. However, the service, which is similar to the leader's soft skills such as "influence and inspiration," was lacking, thus tilting the entire experience towards being bad. Thus the restaurant fell short of making the customer experience a good one. Bottom line: the restaurant failed to make more money and lost the chance to earn repeat customers. Heck, with a good experience we may have even ordered the most expensive dessert on the menu!

What would have changed the entire experience? *Answer*: employees with commitment who brought enthusiasm to their work.

Enthusiasm truly makes all the difference in life. It's present when employees take complete ownership of the job for which they're responsible. Inside the team, employees who work with enthusiasm raise the bar for others as the trait becomes contagious. Externally, customers who come in contact with these employees enjoy their experience with the team and are curious why things are so fantastic at your company. The experience heightens their emotions and puts them in a good mood for the day, thus creating a situation the customer is anxious to repeat.

Why do people like the Olympics and college sports so much? Enthusiasm and passion! These athletes aren't playing for money—instead they're willing to work at their craft and improve their skills because they are passionate about the game. Their excitement is genuine, and their vision is optimistic. As the work of Dr. Martin Seligman indicates, enthusiasm and optimism are contagious. His study of more than half a million children and adults scientifically confirmed two things: (1) optimism makes you more effective at whatever you do, and (2) optimism can be learned.

There is no better example in the past twenty-five years of someone who approached his work with a high degree of enthusiasm than Earvin "Magic" Johnson's playing in the 1980s with the Los Angeles Lakers. His passion for winning was not only a driving force—his enthusiasm for the game was magnetic. His smile showed the fun he was having which made everyone curious as to why he was so excited. Because Johnson's enthusiasm was contagious, the entire city of Los Angeles took on more of a college-town feel.

As Johnson related in an ESPN Classic interview, after his first pro game at the age of twenty in which he passed the ball to Kareem Abdul-Jabbar for a winning last second shot, he ran over to Jabbar, hugged him around his neck, and acted like they'd just won the championship. When Jabbar reminded Magic that this was the first game of the season and they had eighty-one to go, Magic said, "And if you hit a shot like that, I'll be hugging you eighty-one more times!" Now that's someone who went about his work with enthusiasm!

Both co-workers and customers enjoy surrounding themselves with people who have fun, feel passion about what they do, and attack their day with enthusiasm. In this type of environment, people are productive and willing to give more. Yes, skill and talent are important ingredients of success, but more important are employees who view their work responsibilities as their career rather than just a job. There's a huge difference in the productivity level, error rate, customer experience, and employee satisfaction when workers enjoy and are passionate about their jobs.

Leading by example in creating and maintaining a work environment with enthusiasm is vital in building a great organization. The best part of it is that we all control our own level of enthusiasm. The accomplished director, musician, and writer Gordon Parks reminded us that we can turn it on at will: "Enthusiasm is the electricity of life. How do you get it? You act enthusiastic until you make it a habit." As a leader, it is your job to show up to work every morning and supply the energy level you want your staff to emulate.

The Wright Brothers museum in Dayton, Ohio is a grand tribute to the pioneering and courageous spirit of these two men. The museum highlights a story that reinforces how infectious living with enthusiasm can be.

In May 1910 Orville Wright, who invented air travel with his brother Wilbur, took his father Milton Wright on his first and only flight aboard his new invention, the glider plane. The flight lasted nearly seven minutes and rose to about 350 feet. At the height of the ride, do you know what Orville's 82-year-old father yelled to him?

"Higher, Orville, higher!"

Enthusiasm knows no age, sex, or color. It is contagious with people when they know they are on the edge of innovation and greatness.

Knowledge instills Confidence
Confidence instills Enthusiasm
Enthusiasm *Sells*!

Chapter 7

Simple Messages Seep into the Soul

"The more you can inspire your team members to be the best they can be, the further your reach as a leader."
—Jack Welch

Leadership is a well-discussed topic with many facets and points of interest; however, leadership is most effective when it is kept simple and clear. A leader's job can be split into two halves with industry technical expertise and skill on one side and on the other side, the ability to communicate effectively, mobilize employees, and inspire them to give their best efforts.

Truly gifted leaders and public speakers know how to take difficult, complex material and break it down into very manageable, bite-sized chunks of information.

As change management is a central part of a leader's job, it is important to take time not only to ensure all aspects of the material are covered, but to also form the way in which the information will be communicated. When introducing and asking for change, a leader must make an employee's first step towards that change look realistic, attainable, and logical.

A general-to-specific format works well in adapting communication to a specific audience. In focusing in on the general message, it is important to keep that message simple and understandable. Remember, the objective is to invite employees to take a confident, attainable first step towards contributing to the overall goal. The ability to retain information increases as people understand where they fit into the overall goal. As the team members understand their role, it then makes it easier for them to prioritize and execute their tasks for the day.

The first company we will look at to reinforce this point about simple messaging is Pike Place Fish Market in Seattle, WA. At this public market, several fish markets sell the same product, at the same location, to the same customers. As you can imagine, there aren't a ton of ways for a seller to present a compelling value proposition to differentiate itself when it is offering exactly the same thing as the next guy. But they do—which is why this is such a great example of the power of simple practices and simple messaging. Pike Place Fish Market vendors have done such an excellent job in their sales and customer experience techniques that they have books, DVDs, and management consultants teaching their simple yet successful ways. In fact they've become so popular and successful that they're now known as the *World Famous* Pike Place Fish Market!

At the cornerstone of the market are four very simple goals to which the owners hold every employee accountable. Nowhere will you find difficult concepts such as "revenue minus cost analysis," "budget goals," or "earnings before tax analysis." Instead, all four goals focus on the soft skills employees use to enhance the customer's experience. The owners know that if all employees consistently deliver on these goals, the budget will naturally fall into place and the business will produce healthy revenue numbers.

Here are the four customer goals, known as the Fish Philosophy at Pike Place Fish Market:

- **Make Their Day**—do the little things to make their experience special.
- **Be There**—be in the moment and genuine.
- **Choose Your Attitude**—you control it from the minute you arrive at work.
- **Play**—have fun, show enthusiasm for your work.

All four are very simple goals that *any* employee can immediately understand and execute upon. They all directly focus on the employees' abilities to control their actions and emotions, then create a fantastic customer experience knowing that repeat business will naturally follow. This is a very simple philosophy, yet extremely powerful when you think about how many companies *do not* deliver upon these four goals.

The second example to reinforce the power of simple messages comes from the four disciplines of execution taught by management consultant Franklin Covey. Again, we don't see any message regarding numbers, budget, profit margins, or cost structures. What we do see is a need to focus on the employee; to provide clear, actionable messages; and to follow up. This is a good example why leaders must save the "numbers speech" for the accounting departments and CFOs, instead taking the time to tap into the emotions of their team, to bring out the full potential of team members, and to craft their messages so as to be clear, concise, and motivational.

Franklin Covey's four disciplines of execution are:

- Focus on the wildly important—think big and prioritize tasks.
- Create a compelling scoreboard—people react differently when score is being kept.
- Translate lofty goals into specific actions— give your team a clear roadmap.
- Hold each other accountable all of the time— everyone plays by the same rules.   (Covey, 2004)

You can adopt the construction company's "faster, cheaper, better" philosophy from chapter two; my Team Laguna branch values of hard work, mutual respect, and having fun; the Fish Philosophy; or Franklin Covey's four disciplines—or create your own from scratch. The most important action you can take is to reflect on your business and your people and establish a simple message that is easy to understand and remember, but will drive results. Remember: simple messages seep into the soul and allow employees to become tremendous followers of your leadership.

Chapter 8

Connecting Quotes to Your Business Strategy

"The key to communicating is connecting with the audience."
—Lain Chroust Ehmann

Imagine for a moment your day going something like this:

You wake up and head down to Starbucks for a latte, where you run into John F. Kennedy. You then go to the local deli for lunch, and while waiting for your sandwich to be prepared, you have a chat with Thomas Edison and Jackie Robinson. In the afternoon, you stop for gas, and guess what—Amelia Earhart is there doing the same thing! Then on the way home from work, you stop to pick up a pizza for the family and guess who's in front of you? Abraham Lincoln and Thomas Jefferson. You would probably go to sleep thinking you'd had a pretty incredible day with some great conversations.

The good news is that you can have this kind of day whenever you begin to pay attention to what you're facing either personally or in business and take the time to understand the words left behind by the most influential leaders of our nation (or better yet, the world). We are surrounded by famous quotations from our greatest leaders as we can find them in newspapers, magazines, e-mail signature lines, advertisements, movies, documentaries, desk calendars ... heck, I've even seen one on a restaurant menu!

Why are quotations used so often?

Two reasons: one, they provide instant credibility, and two, they get the audience's thoughts going in a specific direction to underscore an idea or point being made. These are golden nuggets of information left for us to use as we wish—leader to leader. However, they are underutilized in today's business world, and more importantly, by leaders who need assistance in delivering messages that are remembered and acted upon. If we respect these men and women for their intelligence, courage, and persistence, then why wouldn't we use the thoughts and ideas they left behind that they believed contributed to their greatness? If they were passionate about some idea and believed it led to their success, shouldn't we take that seriously? Of course we should!

Quotations from our best leaders are a powerful tool and a solid first step towards effective communication. Remember, the objective is to connect with the audience, get people's attention in a creative way, and then expand that message to apply to the work environment or challenge being faced.

As we discussed in chapter five, one component of successful leadership is to establish a vision and to set a course to achieve it. Obviously, e-mailing out a few popular quotations isn't the entire formula for successful leadership. However, connecting with your staff members and drawing out their passion to strive for more or become better is essentially what a leader is there to do. Lain Chroust Ehmann writes in his article "How to Develop the Will and Skill to be a Leader":

> When you have something to say, say it in the simplest way possible. Save the fancy verbal footwork and piles of data for the engineering team, and stick to word pictures and vivid descriptions. (2007, 66)

Many leaders try to be someone they're not or put pressure on themselves to always say something profound when a simple leadership quotation from someone else can be very powerful and effective. In a majority of the meetings where I included a quote and connected it to my business strategy, then asked employees for their reaction to the meeting, they ended up reciting the quote as something they'd retained. It works—try it.

After you select an appropriate quote, the formula to an effective message is customizing it and making it relevant to what you're facing as a team or organization. These messages should be sent out one to two times per week to your entire team. The collections of quotes found at the back of this book are some of my favorites that can be adapted to several broad challenges. I've also included quotes with narratives or messages that I've created and found effective. These were sent out to my staff members to energize, inspire, and motivate them, and ultimately to help set their direction.

Want to get an immediate reaction from your staff and create some positive discussion about how they can become better? Review some of the messages at the back of this book, select a few relevant to your situation, and send them out. Then sit back and see how you begin to build values and a positive culture within your company or department. I guarantee you will get a reaction from your team and that reaction will open positive dialogue.

As creative thoughts and actions tap into the will of your employees, they are an effective way to inspire. There is an art to leadership that touches on your ability to be creative. Political scientist and educator Thomas E. Cronin in his essay "Thinking and Learning about Leadership" ponders whether we can teach people to become leaders as he believes, "Leadership at its best comes close to creativity." (1989, 48) Try your hand at thinking outside the box to develop interesting ways to lead your staff. If you need help or feel you're not a creative person by nature, this book can become a useful resource for you. Momentum is a precious quality for any team. If you get it going in the right direction and have your team behind you, you'll be amazed what you can accomplish!

Matt's Leadership Model

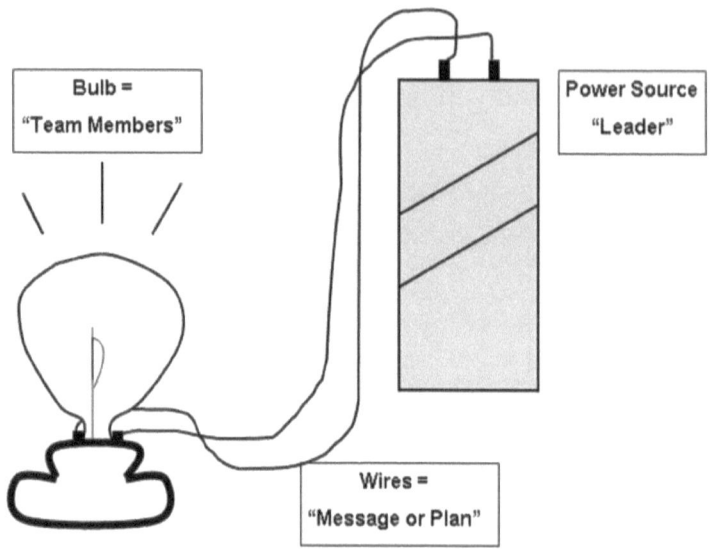

—Matt Modugno, 2008

How Bright is Your Bulb?

This old school science project depicting electricity can teach us quite a bit about the workings of leadership. The power source represents you as the leader, the wires are your message and your plan, and the light bulb itself represents your team members.

All three pieces play equally important roles. The power source must be strong and filled to capacity, the wires must have a direct contact and deliver a clear message, and the bulb must be willing to accept the charge and be lit brightly and consistently over time.

How bright is your bulb? Is the power source running on empty? Are the wires about to short out? Do you have an adequate power source, but the bulb is burned? Or, is everything working OK, but you're only getting twenty watts of light when you know your team is capable of one hundred? All of these questions are directly tied to leadership dilemmas or challenges. Actually, this very analogy can be applied to business leadership as easily as coaching, teaching, or parenting

Leading with Passion is about the "wires"—it shows you how to deliver a clear, simple, and compelling message. However, all three materials must be interdependent if they are to be successful as a whole unit.

A leader's objective becomes simple: light the bulb as brightly as possible for as long as possible. Get a true connection.

Chapter 9

Leading with Passion!

"When people believe in something very deeply, things happen."
—Cesar Chavez

To be a leader you must show passion for your work. The leader sets the tone for the team as well as provides the example of how people should be treated. The way a leader treats his or her staff is most likely the way the staff will treat each other. So, if the leader treats the staff with respect and honesty, the staff will likely treat each other with respect and honesty. Conversely, if the leader is demeaning or manipulative, the staff members will be the same to each other.

Beyond treating people with respect, the question becomes *how do you get your staff to work with the same passion you do?*

The process for building passionate workers who are dedicated and loyal begins with a leader who is *genuine* and *trustworthy*. When a leader is genuine and trustworthy, workers feel safe. When the team members feels safe they are not only willing to give more of themselves to the job, but they also feel comfortable to be creative in finding work solutions. This environment of "reciprocal trust" between leader and team allows your team to deliver its best efforts on a consistent basis.

Trust is to a leader what gas is to a car: if you don't have it, you aren't going anywhere. In 2002, our company polled over one hundred employees and asked them to rank what they considered the most important qualities when considering a job. We gave them a deck of fifty-two cards with the back of each card focusing on a different job quality. Some examples of the qualities listed were compensation, acknowledgement, clear goals, respect, opportunity, consistent feedback, teamwork, promotion, and organization. Do you know what eighty-five percent of the employees desired as their number one work quality? *Trust.*

Trust can be broken in a variety of ways, but in the business world, a common leadership pitfall has to do with the leader's focus and motives. Many businesses, especially small ones, are set up with working managers and working leaders. This means the leader's job isn't merely to lead the team, support the people, and create a vision for the future, but also to produce business and make a living. If not handled correctly, this delicate balance can easily cause team members to think the leader has ulterior motives or a hidden agenda, and may even be out for personal gain. Team members might say things such as:

"Watch out, because he'll throw you under the bus if it means he gets a larger commission."

or

"He's only around until his stock options kick in, and then he's outta here!"

If your team was saying either of these two things about you, do you think it would affect how they worked under you? Would it affect your ability to motivate and inspire your team to greater results? Of course it would! Dale Carnegie urges us to not think only of ourselves. "Don't think only of your needs. Think about George's needs here. Or Sandy's needs there. And think about what kinds of questions you would ask to draw them out, to understand their needs." (1993, 70) Leaders can't mobilize and inspire people without first having a genuine interest in the well-being of their people. Any mixed message or mixed agenda will absolutely halt your chances of having any positive influence over your team. Once a leader violates the team's trust, there's no guarantee that person can ever get it back.

When you connect at a deep level, it becomes motivational. When you motivate people, you get them to deliver their best work. You then begin to see accomplishments they never thought possible. Effective communication leads to passion, passion leads to motivation, motivation leads to enthusiasm, enthusiasm leads to great accomplishments, great accomplishments lead to surpassing budget numbers, and surpassing budget numbers leads to a healthy organization and healthy paychecks for all!

I've always been surprised that presidential nominees including incumbents don't get more creative in the messaging of their beliefs to the citizens. After all, the citizens are their "staff" with whom they must connect. There's a mad dash to connect with people around election time, but that is because the nominee needs something in return... your vote! Why then don't they take a *creative* path towards showing their passion for their work and connecting with the people? For example, why not take up space quarterly in three or four of the largest newspapers across the nation and write a personal memo to the public? They could use it to connect with the people and discuss current events, foreign policy, or challenges facing Congress. They could even take credit for or acknowledge the monumental achievements of others. Imagine going out to the driveway to grab the Sunday newspaper thinking, "I wonder what ole Mr. Bush wants to tell me today?" This would be cost effective and wide reaching. Talk about presidents staying *connected* with their audience in a *genuine* way and improving their approval rating.

You will know you were successful when you've made true breakthroughs with team members, changed their days from bad to good, altered their perspectives on a challenge, or coached them through an employees spat. Here are a few real-world examples that validate this leadership style and show how my team and I grew together:

An employee response after I sent out a motivational quote on the power of having a positive attitude.

"Attitude will determine everything! The interesting thing about attitude is that as an individual, I choose it. It is not something that is forced on me. Circumstances will come my way that I cannot control; however, I can control how I react to them. This was a fantastic quote that you sent at the just right time. Thank you for your 'Thought of the Day!'"

—Mark Mendenhall, Account Executive

An employee's response after I sent out a message on giving maximum effort and continuing to polish skills to be the best.

"WOW! Thank you for forwarding such a simple but powerful statement!

"I was about to call you today because I'm just not feeling it. My managers are checked-out and I have not been feeling it for over a week. I believe in our company so much, but feel like I am holding on to false hope. I hate not believing in what I have to sell, so I have not really been selling. But after reading this message, I thought,

'Hell, I always sell myself first, why would I not today!' So, I'm going out to the field today!

"Thanks, Matt! You made me smile!"

—Mercedes Torres, Account Executive

A leadership coach's comments on how the leadership style mentioned in this book produces results.

"Matt possesses the unique combination of being technically savvy as well as exhibiting phenomenal relational skills ... His understanding of what makes his workforce tick and how to develop his people so that they are in position to take on more extensive and complex roles and responsibilities are manifested in visible and varied ways. What a great person to work with!"

—Lee Hayward, Leadership & Development, Hayward & Associates—San Jose, CA

Steve Jobs, CEO of Apple Computer, said that being fired from Apple was one of the best things that happened to him. He explained, "It freed me to enter one of the most creative periods in my life." In June 2005, he stood in Stanford Stadium in Palo Alto, California, and conveyed some simple yet powerful lessons while giving the commencement address:

I'm convinced that the only thing that kept me going was that I loved what I did. You've got to find what you love. Your work is going to fill a large part of your life, and the only way to be truly satisfied is to do what you believe is great work. And the only way to do great work is to love what you do. If you haven't found it yet, keep looking. Don't settle.

There is no question about it: the best leaders show *passion* and *genuine* interest in the work they do every day.

A leader's ability to connect with his or her staff and create clear, actionable messages change the way the employees go about their day. Even just a nudge from a leader can change a team's effort from mediocre to maximum. These skills may seem simple or insignificant; however, most of the time it is the small things that get done that take a company from being good to being great. As the leader, *you* are responsible to recognize these moments and act! Every time my name was mentioned in the above comments, it was really a validation of my team and what we were able to accomplish together under one value system to which I held everyone accountable.

Chapter 10

Breaking Bread Together

"You can accomplish anything in life,
provided that you do not mind who gets the credit."
—Harry S. Truman

Next to being trustworthy, a leader's most important attribute is the ability to be genuine in their dealings, feelings, and conversations. Along those same lines, a leader can't miss the opportunity to celebrate team success together or acknowledge individuals for their accomplishments. People remember who went out of their way to remember them as they reached a pinnacle in their career. These represent golden moments for leaders to show they care—that they are genuinely interested in the success of the team and its people.

Areas to track and navigate that are personal to your staff are things such as employee growth over the year, career-best achievements, or just the anniversary of someone joining the company. For a newcomer, it may be being the quickest to a sales benchmark. These are all personal categories that show you are paying attention and are concerned about people's individual successes as well as those of the office as a whole. Calling or sending an e-mail to acknowledge an event in any of these categories shows you're a thoughtful leader who is paying attention.

As a leader, no office gathering should be beneath your attendance. You should go to everything from office birthday celebrations to baby showers, going away parties, and dinner celebrations. This shows you are committed with all your being to the team and genuinely interested in your employees' lives, not just their work contributions. You must show you are human and open yourself up to your team. However, don't bother attending these gatherings if it is not a genuine action that comes from the heart.

As a leader, you can't have a selfish bone in your body. You are there to do a job and build a team, not your bank account. Leaders who are out for themselves can't gain the support of their teams and won't bring out the group's full potential. Leaders have a strong personal will to get to the top of the mountain and they are very driven people, but they must also have a desire to get to that top with their entire team. Better yet, the best of leaders want their teams to get to the top of the mountain first as they go back to check to make sure nobody got left behind. Harry Truman reinforced this point when he said:

"You can accomplish anything in life, provided that you do not mind who gets the credit."

Another way to break bread together and show your genuine interest in the well-being of your teammates is to conduct training classes to help polish their skills. Most leaders have traveled a road from which others could benefit and learn. By the time I held an influential leadership role, I had almost ten years of experience under my belt and had worked a variety of positions. By designing courses from an introductory level to advanced skills training, I was able to connect with all of my teammates and demonstrate my desire to assist them in furthering their careers. At the same time, I was able to clearly identify my team members' talents which gave me a roadmap for future planning.

I hear many leaders say, "I just need to lead by example and show my team what's required to be successful." While this is true, it cannot become your sole leadership strategy. Effective leadership is not that simple. If it were, what would happen when an employee didn't do a job well? To lead by example, would the leader need to step in and finish that job? No, as this would take the leader away from his or her duties. All of a sudden, the boat would veer off course. When I think of leading by example, I think of leaders who live what they preach, who adhere to the team values they create, and who treats people in the way they want the team members to treat each other. Leading by example means there are no double standards and no hypocrisy between the leader and the team.

Arthur Ashe, a world-class tennis player, offered us a simple yet interesting perspective in leadership shortly before his death. In October 1992, in a PBS interview on *The Charlie Rose Show*, he said the personality trait of leading by example begins at home between us and our children.

"My wife and I talk about this with our six-year old daughter. Children are much more impressed by what they see you do than by what you say. Children at that age certainly keep you honest. If you have been preaching one thing all along and all of a sudden you don't do it, they're going to bring it right up in your face."

"I tell her it's not polite to eat with your elbows on the table. Then after dinner I'm putting my elbows up. She says, 'Daddy, your elbows are on the table.' You have to be man enough or woman enough, to say, 'You're right, and take your elbows down. In fact, that's an even stronger learning experience than her hearing it. It means that she did listen in the past. She understands it. And, she recognizes it when she sees it."

Each time Ashe said "children" or "her," replace that with "my team." Then replace the action of "elbows on the table" with any value you are trying to impress upon your team. Now, reread Ashe's comments with these changes. Do you see how the leader and team need to follow the same rules? Ashe gives us a very simple reminder of how important staying true to yourself and your values and leading by example can be to leaders who want to have an impact with their teams.

As there are many benefits in taking a genuine interest in your team, the next time a baby shower shows up on your calendar, make sure you lead by example and attend!

Chapter 11

You Get What You Measure

"Life is only as complicated as we choose to make it."
—Matt Modugno

The farming industry has the saying, *you reap what you sow*. Planting seeds in the spring allows you to feast in the fall and winter. The general lesson here shows the value of thinking ahead and being proactive so that you can benefit later. Similarly, in the field of leadership you must also plan ahead by creating a proactive strategy to achieve your goals. It is essential to set aside time to think about the critical areas to your success and to design a strategy to highlight those with your team. An even more important task is to filter out what is truly *critical* from those areas that are only *important*, and then what is important from those areas that are *time wasters*. This hierarchy of task importance will help you frame your strategy and simplify your message to your team.

I strongly believe you will get what you measure, so it really becomes a question of *what do you want to measure?* and, *are you measuring the right things to reach paramount success?* If your team members are the "doers" of work, then you as the leader must be the thinker, designer, and planner. As your team begins to produce, you better be measuring the right things to be successful!

There is a sweet spot in selecting the number of areas you want to measure, one that rests between selecting too few areas and too many. If you select too few, the measurement may not adequately reflect what needs to be done to achieve healthy results. If you select too many areas, you run the risk of confusing or demoralizing your team as it may be close to impossible to deliver good results in all of them.

I'm a strong believer that the sweet spot lives between creating three to five goals. You should be able to boil down the most vital areas to your team's success within these parameters. The fewer the better as this will enable you to focus your team's energy very exactly. It will also help simplify your communication to your team while leaving little room for misinterpretation.

For example, in parenting our children, my wife and I have boiled down our expectations to two simple areas. We preach to them that *respect* and *responsibility* will equal *freedom*. Respect entails how they treat others such as their classmates, siblings, grandparents, teachers, etc. Responsibility covers doing their chores and homework, maintaining good personal hygiene, and honoring commitments. We tell them if they take care of the two R's, they will earn the freedom to do almost anything they want to do. What we are measuring covers a lot of ground, yet it is very easy for them to remember and execute upon.

In chapters three and seven we looked at establishing core values that focused on driving behaviors. Besides shaping behaviors and attitudes, leaders need to measure and drive performance. So, when looking at your team's performance what do you want to measure? Here are a few suggestions universal to any business team:

- Productivity
- Quality
- Revenue
- Costs
- Profit margin
- Customer service
- Culture/Employee satisfaction
- Manufacturing speed
- Sales growth
- Sales closed
- Sales milestones
- Operations efficiency
- Errors
- Training
- Attendance

Most organizations will likely monitor all of these categories; however, for day-to-day "dashboard-like" messages to your team, you should be able to boil this down to between three to five goals. When you bring awareness to an issue, you are showing it's a vital area to the success of the team. When you want to move the needle in a specific area, it is important to measure where the team is currently, set a benchmark for where you want to go, and track that measure for daily and weekly performance. It can be treated as a journey of going from point A to point B. Set milestones so that you can celebrate successes along the way.

Recently, on a sunny San Diego day around lunch time I had the urge for a fish taco. I went to our local taco shop and placed my order. When I heard my name called I went to the counter to pick up my meal and noticed a receipt with my name on it. Upon a closer look, I noticed the following words on my receipt—Prep Time: 2 min 1 secs.

They were measuring the time it took from taking my order to the time it took to prepare it. It was their manufacturing time from placing an order to fulfillment. What a brilliant idea in taking a very simple measure and cascading it down throughout the taco shop. The leadership team members understood this to be central to their customer service level and have probably attached employee rewards to it for maintaining certain turn-time goals.

At my office, in 2003 our team wanted to improve the depth of business we were receiving per account. We came up with a measure called account penetration. This was the total number of loans we closed divided by the number of broker offices that closed loans with us. For example, three hundred loans closed divided by eighty broker offices equals 3.75 loans per broker office. I then raised awareness of the importance of this new measure, set a benchmark of where we wanted to be, and followed up each week with performance updates. We also made this number a bit more personal by running reports illustrating each salesperson's penetration number. The theory here was that if all people improved their individual numbers, the branch's numbers would automatically become healthy. It was an individual message to each employee that rolled up to an overall branch goal. The results were fantastic, and within a few short months my office led all offices across the nation in account penetration. I got what I measured!

As a leader, you need to be prepared to take responsibility for the failures of the team as much as the successes. Choosing the right areas to monitor is like selecting the right numbers on a combination lock. There are many different combinations you can try, but ultimately you need to find the one that works. Think of it this way: A basketball coach might tell his team that if they outrebound the opponent, they will certainly win the game. They then go out and get more rebounds than their opponent, but nonetheless lose. Whose fault is it? *Answer:* the coach's! It is the coach's fault because he designed a failed strategy. He may have done his homework and truly believed the game could be won by outrebounding the opponent, but he focused his team's energy behind the wrong goal, and it turned out to be a losing strategy, thus it's not the players' fault. This is an example of a failed plan that can easily happen in the business world as it does on the basketball court. As a leader, you have a responsibility to do your homework and select the right goals for your team to pursue because *you will get what you measure.*

Chapter 12

Three Cardinal Sins of Leadership

"Confidence shared is better than confidence only in yourself."
—_Mike Krzyzewski_

This book defines leadership and explains my leadership experiences. As is true of anything we attempt to define in life, often it is helpful to take a different perspective by looking at _what something is not._ Let's take a look at the "dark side" of leadership, including the areas in which leaders most commonly stumble. By doing so and contemplating what leadership is not, we will achieve more insight on what effective leaders need to avoid.

By now, it should be apparent to you that becoming an effective leader is no easy task as it requires a combination of strategic skills in understanding the technical side of your business and the ability to connect, influence, and coach others. I believe these skills can be learned; however, some individuals master them more quickly simply because of their innate strengths. Some people intuitively understand business strategies and the tactics behind them, while others are born with magnetic personalities and find it easy to lead others. All of these innate talents can assist you in a leadership role.

Highly effective leaders are *not* people who are reactive more than proactive, poor at rallying employees around a cause, refuse to have an open door policy, miss opportunities to acknowledge a job well done, fail to teach employees to look at challenges with a deeper perspective of the business, lack confidence, don't allow themselves to be vulnerable, and aren't humble and genuine. If this sounds like your boss, find a new one immediately as that person isn't leading you anywhere. Here's a closer look at the top three cardinal sins of leadership:

Cardinal Sin of Leadership #1: *Violation of trust*

The first cardinal sin of leadership can be defined as a *violation of trust.* The level of trust between leaders and their teams is the Holy Grail of successful leadership—the point from which all things flow. Try executing strategies without a foundation of trust and you'll find failure real fast. As mentioned earlier in chapter nine, leaders can break trust with their teams in a variety of ways such as using their current job as a springboard to another, showing favoritism towards certain employees, or needing personal success instead of team success. Employees may even watch how their leader treats vendors or clients for clues as to how the leader genuinely treats people. Bad experiences are magnified and can cause long-term damage to a leader's image and style.

We can draw a similar comparison when looking at the world of sales. When a sales rep completes a solid transaction and delivers a positive customer experience, the rep will be lucky if the customer remains loyal for one week and shares the positive experience with one person. Conversely, customers who have had just one bad experience will likely feel the need to share that experience with their entire office. They will want to tell their friends how bad the experience was and ensure you get little or no future business! It will take at least five great experiences in the future for the customer to clean the slate and forget the bad experience with you. This is assuming you get a second chance, and if you do, it may take months to "re-earn" the right to the customer's business. A customer's resiliency to good and bad experiences looks something like this:

One good customer experience—Lasts one week and the customer may tell one person about it.

One bad customer experience—Takes five good ones to offset one bad one, and the customers may tell their entire office about what you did to them!

The pitfalls of leadership are no different. Once you violate trust, fairness, and mutual respect, you virtually kill your chances of being an effective leader. The cohesiveness of the group breaks down and people become more interested in looking out for themselves instead of the team.

Cardinal Sin of Leadership #2: *Failure to admit areas of weakness*

The second cardinal sin of leadership occurs when the *leader's ego* blinds the leader against looking introspectively to address weaknesses. Very few leaders have *all* the tools to be an effective leader, and even if they do, it is still not appropriate for them to think no other opinion is worthy of consideration. The majority of leaders out there have weaknesses as well as strengths.

Your first step is to take an honest look at yourself and analyze what you're good at and where you need help. It's very likely the areas in which you are good are those in which you have always been good, and your areas of weaknesses are those with which you have always struggled. Over time, you've probably become aware of these things so they don't come as a surprise. The key is to be honest with yourself and to go about building your team to offset the areas in which you are weak. Know your strengths, but spend more time addressing your weaknesses.

Like all of us, our recognized leaders have been human beings with both strengths and weaknesses. Past U.S. presidential leaders provide good examples of this dichotomy. Michael Genovese, chair of Leadership Studies at Loyola Marymount University, writes in his work *Memo to a New President*:

For a U.S. presidential leader to be effective, one needs the vision of John F. Kennedy, the political skills of Lyndon Johnson, the strategic insight of Richard Nixon, the genuineness of Gerald Ford, the character of Jimmy Carter, the charisma of Ronald Reagan, the experience of George H. W. Bush, and the interpersonal skills of Bill Clinton. (2008, 225)

If the people listed above had to be aware of their weaknesses, why should you be any different? The key is to know *yourself* and *your style*, but more importantly, to be *humble* enough to acknowledge your weaknesses and find ways to lessen them.

Cardinal Sin of Leadership #3: *Failure to balance democracy and dictatorship*

The third cardinal sin is failure to recognize the balance between a *democracy* and a *dictatorship*. In a business environment, a pendulum that swings too far in either direction can be problematic for a leader. A work environment that has a dominant leader, one who enjoys "running the show" in a classic dictatorship style, may be at serious risk of demoralizing the staff. A strong top-down dictator structure does not encourage creative thought that can lead to increased efficiency. This "silo management style" ends up being very much one-sided with ideas that can improve the team getting lost or squashed by the leader. It is important to find ways to disintegrate department or division boundaries to get people to work better together across the firm. Designing a broader management team that reports to the leader will foster an environment where silos are harder to develop.

On the other hand, a work environment that is too democratic runs the risk of failing to have a vision behind which its efforts can be aligned. Leaders who are overly concerned about gathering a consensus before moving ahead may be too idealistic in their thoughts. The work environment will likely be chaotic and confusing, resulting in a lack of direction. This is where the phrase "analysis to paralysis" comes from. It's unlikely any team will always agree 100 percent on all decisions, so a person who chases that success rate is not leading at all.

Instead, the goal should be a careful blend of the two styles. Leaders must involve others in their decisions, but once they have enough information, they must have the fortitude to make the final decision that moves the organization forward.

One of the best and most productive meetings I ever conducted happened when I invited common, everyday line workers to our strategy meetings. Usually these quarterly meetings were reserved for managers and executives, but inviting workers from within the "trenches" gave this meeting new life. We were able to realize issues occurring on the front lines and the worker was able to see dilemma's facing our future. I think we *all* came out of those meetings better employees.

Chapter 13

Your Wireless Connection

"The most important single ingredient in the formula of success is knowing how to get along with people."
—*Theodore Roosevelt*

After returning home from a three-day vacation, my daughter Samantha exclaimed, "Daddy, oh my gosh, I have seventy-eight emails!" Similarly, there were times I'd return to work after four or five days off and have upwards of four hundred emails to sift through and return. At times our wireless devices can feel suffocating. With the invention of the personal computer and the Internet, Bill Gates and the wireless world thrust our society into the future by one hundred years or more. Can you imagine how different your world would be today without your PC, Mac, or the Internet? Monumental inventions such as the automobile, airplane, and computer completely changed the way society works and plays.

Specifically, the Internet is responsible for bringing us information at any time and at any location. With it, there are no "business hours" we need to work within as it gives us full 24/7 access to information. We can enjoy our morning bagel at our favorite shop while researching ancient history or learning about an illness with which a loved one has been diagnosed. The rate at which information moves today is truly remarkable.

The Internet has sparked the creativity of entrepreneurs and opened the door to many new businesses. Consumers can now make purchases across the nation at places they never before could access immediately. You can create a virtual store filled with digital photos of your merchandise, connect to PayPal for billing and UPS for delivery, and whoosh—just like that, you're up and running!

Slowly, we're becoming a society of individuals who depend less and less on a network of other people. We look up history, buy merchandise, trade stocks, take online classes, develop businesses, balance checkbooks, investigate our children's illnesses, and coordinate trips all without needing any human interaction. And I thought losing my bank teller to an ATM meant I was becoming a less social person!

So, you ask, *what does this have to do with leadership?*

Recently, our company went through a major reduction in force due to a slowdown in the mortgage industry. I asked one of the sales managers I highly respected what he might be interested in doing now that he was no longer with the firm. He said that after twelve-plus years in the business, he didn't want to call on customers anymore. Instead he wanted to develop an Internet business, connect to PayPal, and begin to watch the money start flowing in! In essence, he was telling me he wanted to unplug from his leadership role and become responsible only for himself. I felt as though I'd lost a good soldier, one who was becoming an excellent sales manager and beginning to grow his ability to coach and direct others. He was connecting with his sales staff and polishing his leadership skills, making him more influential. However, the business opportunity to isolate himself on the Internet was more intriguing to him.

Although we aren't losing all of our potential great leaders, the wireless world creates opportunities for good leaders to become isolated and detached from their network of people. Going forward, we need to be aware of this and ensure we continue to grow and harvest the leaders of tomorrow. We can't lose touch or stop practicing how to connect with people, build teams, communicate effectively, motivate, inspire, or solve problems. As leaders, these are our biggest assets, and they must continue to be practiced regularly.

Michael A. Genovese adds the following in his book, *Memo to a New President:*

> Leadership is a process of influence wherein the leader helps propel the group toward the attainment of some mutually desirable good ....The tools of leadership are there. It is up to you to learn how to use them creatively and artfully. (2008, 33,35)

Prior to the Internet and the information superhighway it created, Walt Disney reminded us of the leader's responsibility of connecting with employees one by one. Later in Walt's life, a boy asked him if he still drew Mickey Mouse. Walt told the boy that he didn't any longer as several studio animators were responsible for that now. The little boy paused and then asked, "Well then, Mr. Disney, just what do you do?" Walt smiled and replied:

> Sometimes I think of myself as a little bee. I go from one area of the studio to another and gather pollen and sort of stimulate everybody. I guess that's the job I do. (Isbouts, 2001, 4)

Walt was no longer a *doer* of work, but was now in a leadership role where connecting with people and trading ideas were his greatest contributions to the team. Walt's "pollen" was the creative ideas from across his company, and the "stimulation" was his leadership influence and inspiration of those ideas. The wireless world will continue to invite a work ethic of isolation; however, a leader's job will always involve connecting with and mobilizing people. Your wireless devices should *enhance* your leadership abilities, not *replace* them.

Chapter 14

Perspective

"I only hope that we don't lose sight of one thing—that it was all started by a mouse."
— *Walt Disney*

Throughout my office we had the typical whiteboards that tracked things such as monthly production, errors, and year-over-year growth. However, the board that generated the most questions and interest was one tucked at the back of the office. It was four feet by three feet with the word *Perspective* at the top. The middle of the board had this observation:

Our company was started in a garage in San Jose, CA with $10,000 of borrowed money. Remember where you came from.
(Followed by four logo graphics that covered the company's twenty-five-year history).

This type of information was grounding and humbling, but it also offered a deep perspective to employees whether they'd been with us for fifteen years or only six months. It encouraged all employees to take pride and ownership in the organization in which they worked. As employee turnover occurred and we needed to welcome new people to the company, sometimes we forgot to tell them our history. In a small way, this board gave employees immediate perspective into the company of which they were a part.

Ken Blanchard, co-author of *The Power of Ethical Management*, talks about the five P's of ethical power for individuals: purpose, pride, patience, persistence, and perspective. He says perspective is at the center of the five P's where someone can oversee others. Blanchard sums this topic up nicely:

> When (you) can achieve perspective your purpose becomes increasingly clear. Perspective brings us full circle back to our purpose ... every problem can be solved if you take some quiet time to reflect, seek guidance, and put things into perspective. (1988, 79)

As a leader, it is important to give your team a bigger picture about the industry and organization in which they work. Leaders are allowed access to information the team doesn't have, which may create a separation in the understanding of the challenges they may be facing. When the leader needs to make decisions, the team may not fully understand why the path chosen is the best one. Providing a dose of perspective can help close that gap.

For example, I offered a training class that focused on the understanding of and dissecting of our monthly profit and loss statement. I shared as much information as I could so the team could see where our office made money and where we spent it. People then started suggesting ways to save money on things such as how often we used couriers and how much paper we needed. It became an eye-opener to all, and I'd like to believe everyone began to take a little more ownership in our office.

Offering a little perspective is really about opening the minds of your team to see the bigger picture and assisting them in connecting the dots on why a certain course must be taken. In essence, you're giving your team the tools to work and think on their own towards the common goals of the organization. Steve Gilliland, CEO of Performance Plus Professional Development, Inc., a company dedicated to training, developing, and improving people worldwide, offers a powerful analogy on the value of injecting perspective into your team. He says:

> I have always operated from the premise that you must focus on the big picture and let others worry about the details. Leaders focus on the forest while managers focus on the trees. As a leader you have to cut through all the fog and smoke and identify what the key issues are. When you do this your subordinates (followers) feel encouraged that they are making progress. Priorities can be set and directives given because the leader sees the big picture. (2004, 2)

As a leader if you ever feel you've gone offtrack, spending some time reflecting on the core of what's truly important can create some constructive thoughts. The solution is to provide some perspective to the challenge you face.

The best speech I've ever heard as it relates to bringing focus to those things that are truly important was Jim Valvano's at the 1993 ESPY Awards. Valvano was the recipient of the Arthur Ashe Courage Award. Here was a man whose fate was determined, as due to cancer, he had just a few months to live, yet he conveyed one of the best messages of all time. In his ten-minute speech, he talked about the three things he felt were most important in life and on which he tried to focus every day. He said we should all focus on *where we started from, where we are,* and *where we want to be someday.* Valvano then posed a question that we all tend to ask ourselves and offered this perspective:

> How do you go from where you *are* to where you *want to be?*
>
> I think you have to have an enthusiasm for life, you have to have a dream, a goal, and you have to be willing to work for it.

In a leadership position, you are immediately a coach and mentor. You must rise to the occasion and embrace this role. Looking at the rich history of your organization and expressing your strategy for success can be very inspirational. Sharing as much information as you can is something employees respect, and it gives them the perspective to be "in your shoes." When a leader offers this type of perspective, the team receives a message of honesty and straight-forwardness—a message that is very grounding.

Another way to gain perspective to your surroundings is to focus on those areas you and your team *can control* instead of wasting time on those things you *cannot control.* When you have this mindset, you think through things much more clearly, but more importantly you become more effective. Suddenly, you will get more out of your day, and you will allow things that normally derail you to pass by almost unnoticed. Take a look at these lists and reflect on your day-to-day activities:

Things you *can* control	Things you *cannot* control
Your work ethic and work quality	Your boss, co-workers, customers, family members, coach
Your attitude	Your company goals or expectations
Your ability to embrace change	Your compensation plan
Your schedule, business plan, strategy	The traffic or weather
Your budget — costs, expenses	The market — rates, stocks, gas prices, etc.

Does this resemble *your* mindset? If not, why?

Are you spending the majority of your day focusing on the items you can control?

Are you spending a very *little* amount of time on those things you cannot control?

This is a very simple test that you can apply to everyday life. Paying closer attention to your reactions and attempting to funnel them into the right direction will make you more effective. Gaining this perspective in your life can lead to less stress, less guilt, less wasted time, and allow you to more fully enjoy life.

Chapter 15

Leaders Among Us

"When you enjoy the journey, everything else is downhill."
—*Clyde Drexler*

At times it seems as though society places a *net worth* requirement on who we accept as leaders. Subconsciously, we might believe a leader is someone who needs to be financially successful, lives in a big house, drives an incredible car, or is able to throw money around carelessly. We feel comfortable following people who appear to have "made it" themselves.

But sadly, this is a mistake. Our vision becomes blurred as to what we should be looking for in a leader. The fact of the matter is that we can see examples of solid leadership every day in various ways all around us that have nothing to do with financial success. In society today, when the word leadership comes up in conversation we immediately think about business leaders or politicians. I believe the word leadership must become a word used in every day conversations because it can be expanded to life's every day achievements. In different ways, we are all leaders in our lives. Some are parents, some are managers, some are public service leaders, teachers, coaches, and some are leaders for their families.

Reflect on four or five people who have had an impact in your life and/or whose contributions to society you respect. Why have they had an impact in your life? How have they left an impression? Why do you respect them and their contributions?

When I think about these questions and apply them to my life, a few names immediately come to mind. Here's a brief look at a few who have left an impression on me including what set them apart as leaders:

Leah Fay

Leah spent a good deal of her life as an educator. She was my seventh and eighth grade algebra teacher. Besides having a friendly demeanor and being a very good communicator, Leah was extremely organized and had a terrific knack for breaking down difficult concepts into easy-to-understand pieces. Why was she so successful? She put in the hard work to make learning fun and different. She made it incredibly easy for her students to take that first step towards wanting to learn and get better. Because of the passion she showed for her job, her students wanted to deliver their best work. As a result, her classes had higher average scores than others in the school district.

Father Bill Moore

Father Bill Moore is one of the most creative people I have crossed paths with in my life. He was my religion teacher at Bishop Alemany High School in Mission Hills, CA. Back in the early 1980s, he was doing things on a chalkboard that only a PowerPoint "drawing toolbar" could rival today. His "out of the box" approach to teaching included the use of colored chalk to highlight his lectures and underscore his messages. By the end of our forty-five minute class, Father Bill's chalkboard looked more like a painting with almost every color of the rainbow accounted for. His willingness to be a creative leader and to develop new ways to communicate earned him the audience's undivided attention and admiration.

While doing research for this book, I reconnected with Bill. It brought a smile to my face to see he'd followed his passion and now has an online art gallery. Keep working with the colored chalk, Father Bill!

Tony, the UPS man

In Mark Sanborn's book, *The Fred Factor*, he explains how his postman Fred went above and beyond the call of duty to deliver exceptional service. Sanborn sums up Fred's impact:

When others might see delivering mail as

monotonous drudgery, Fred sees an opportunity to make a difference in the lives of those he serves ....To this day, I can't tell you what motivated Fred. I know he didn't get paid more for his extraordinary work [and] I doubt he received any special recognition from his employer. (2004, inside flap) My "Fred" is Tony, our area UPS man. When Tony delivers packages to our street, it's not uncommon for him to talk with the neighborhood kids or stop to shoot a few baskets with his delivery gloves still on. Tony doesn't merely leave the package on the doorstep, ring the bell and leave like most do. He waits until you answer the door to say hello and ask how everyone is doing. Two weeks after I first met him, his personalized service was evident when he surprised me by remembering and calling me by my first name. For Tony, obviously the personal interaction and connection is an important ingredient of the way he views a job well done. Fred and Tony share the same passion for their work because they are willing to do the small things that make it fun for them and special for others.

Father Nicholas Dempsey

Growing up and going to Catholic schools meant that I have attended and continue to attend Sunday mass. This also means I've listened to and observed many priests' public speaking abilities. While there is no prerequisite that a priest be a good public speaker, those who have the ability to captivate their congregations can make a huge impact on how their message is received and carried out.

Father Nicholas Dempsey, pastor of St. Therese of Carmel in San Diego, is a true gem when it comes to connecting with his audience. He is a master storyteller who relates true life stories to the Biblical messages he is attempting to deliver. He is also known to bring in props to enhance his communication. I can remember the time he used a lemon tree branch to explain the nurturing required for life to grow. His use of metaphors and storytelling make his messages tangible as well as interesting.

Ashley Falls School - San Diego, CA

Each school year, I attend the standard parent-teacher conferences to discuss my kids' progress. I've come to the conclusion the fourth and fifth grades are a pivotal time for teaching the habits kids will have for a lifetime. Their schoolwork becomes more demanding, the bar of expectation rises, and the free time and parties of first and second grade no longer exist. Instead the teachers strongly emphasize being organized and responsible, developing writing and speaking skills, and acting as a good citizen to others. These transitional years are critical to students forming a solid foundation so that good habits can be developed for years to come.

When I attend a parent-teacher conference, the first thing I look for are the ways in which the teacher *rewards, disciplines, and communicates.* These critical areas are no different than those needed to run a multimillion dollar company. CEOs and their executive team must also define how they will reward, discipline, and communicate. Therefore, a lot can be learned from our teachers and school structure. For example, the teachers at Ashley Falls School in San Diego, CA, are incredibly creative and efficient. As per the California Department of Education, Ashley Falls highly exceeded the state's average in the 2005 California Standards Tests (CST). Eighty-three percent of the Ashley Falls students achieved a proficient or advanced level while the state's average was only thirty-five percent. In addition, Ashley Falls received the honor of the 2008 California Distinguished School Award from the Department of Education.

These everyday leaders offer us prime examples of how everyone should approach work. They are all wildly successful at their jobs because of the passion they show towards them. The common denominators that make them all effective leaders are the following critical points:

- They show a *genuine* interest in the people they lead. They show they *care.*
- They *enjoy* their work and are willing to go the extra mile.

- They have *fun* and seek *creative* ways to teach and communicate.
- They have found a communication style that *works*.

Now, these individuals may not be the next CEOs of Fortune 500 companies, but the effort and leadership qualities they put into their work are both rare and admired. They represent the small minority of effective leaders in America today. Our jobs as leaders in our own communities are to ensure these traits are present within the *majority* of society. As Mark Sanborn sums up, "[They are] a gold plated example of what personalized service look[s] like and a role model for anyone who want[s] to make a difference in his or her work." (2004, inside flap)

These are all living examples of effective leadership in motion. The individuals mentioned had an impact on my life because they *cared* enough about their jobs to do them to the *best of their abilities*. Leadership is not about money, prestige, or titles—it is about having a desire to be *your best*, taking a creative approach in delivering your message to your team, and helping people reach their true potential just as these teachers, UPS man, and pastor do every day. The simplicity of effective leadership was no better summarized than by Hollywood icon Paul Newman who once said, "You just have to do good, and you have to think well, and you have to be concerned about people who have less than you have. I guess I do have more credits than debits in my life."

Make certain that you go out of your way to recognize those individuals who deliver solid leadership skills in your community. Don't observe these skills and keep it to yourself. Celebrate good leadership skills when you see them!

Chapter 16

Stop the Ordinary, Start the Extraordinary

"To lead is to serve: If a guy gives you 5 bucks,
you give him 7 bucks worth of work."
—Bill Russell

Employees naturally fear being called into their boss's office because most of the time, this means there's a problem. Automatically they start thinking about what they did wrong, if they are being let go, or what someone might have said about them.

As a leader, you must erase this notion that being called into your office is a bad thing. Leaders must be approachable because they depend upon employee input to do their jobs better. An employee can be invited into a leader's office for a quick brainstorming session regarding a current office challenge, a positive acknowledgment of hitting a quota or personal best, or a discussion of career aspirations (an immediate favorite topic of any employee). A leader should be conscious of the negative connotation that being called into the office represents and have the desire to change that.

Yet too many times I've seen leaders stumble by blending two messages when they have an employee in their office. First they praise the employee on meeting a certain goal, but then slam the person with a problem, error, or interpersonal issue.

Take a guess what the employee thinks when leaving the office?

You guessed it: the person remembers the problem, error, or interpersonal issue and completely discounts or forgets the message of praise. The leader fails to effectively deliver either message because the two are woven together into one. What the employee retains after a coaching session, meeting, or performance evaluation is squarely dependent upon the effectiveness of the leader's message.

Here's the solution: Don't combine a praise message with a disciplinary message. Keep them separate, and take the necessary time to discuss them both at different meetings. The effectiveness of the message and the employee's retention of the topics discussed will skyrocket.

In addition to conveying direct, effective messages, a leader needs to keep the lines of communication open and welcome any and all input. A leader who does not take the time to open the lines of communication and gather staff feedback is creating a dictatorship, not a democratic environment. Leading with an iron fist has several deficiencies including employee disengagement.

What would you rather have? Team members who work *your* business plan at 50 percent of their potential, or a business plan they had input in creating and on which they deliver 110 percent of their potential?

The answer is simple, yet many leaders fail to realize this important point. When people feel they have had input into creating a goal, they immediately take ownership in delivering the results. Stifling a person's ability to offer creative input produces someone who becomes demoralized and less productive. (By the way, this simple rule works in parenting as well as leading a business).

One of my favorite essays written on effective leadership ideas comes from the *Harvard Business Review on Breakthrough Leadership*. As William H. Peace writes in his essay, "The Hard Work of Being a Soft Manager," essential leadership ingredients are candor, openness, and vulnerability married with hard choices and responsible follow-up. This essay makes clear that soft management does not mean being lax or indecisive, but presents a simple question of whether leaders will get more out of their teams through arrogance, aggressiveness, insensitivity, and a need to always be right versus creating an environment characterized by respect, openness, honesty, and thoughtful intelligence.

A story about humility and class that highlights soft leadership skills is a personal interaction Fred Wilpon, the president of the New York Mets baseball team, had with one of his employees. One afternoon Wilpon was leading a group of school children on a tour of Shea Stadium. He took them in the team dugouts and the clubhouse, then let them stand behind home plate. His final stop was the stadium bull pen where the pitchers warm up. He was stopped by a security guard who was unaware of who Wilpon was and who told him the bull pen wasn't open to the public.

Now, Fred Wilpon certainly had the power to get what he wanted right then and there by flashing his top-level security pass. He could have made the security guard feel small and insignificant for not recognizing who he was, the president of the baseball team. Instead, Wilpon led the students to the far side of the stadium and took them into the bull pen through another gate.

Why did he bother to do that? Wilpon didn't want to embarrass the security guard. The man was doing his job and doing it well. Later that afternoon, Wilpon sent off a handwritten note thanking the guard for showing such concern. The guard felt great about the compliment and you can bet he'll recognize Wilpon the next time the two of them happen to meet.

In his book *The Leader In You*, Dale Carnegie says "Fred Wilpon is a leader not just because of the title he holds or the salary he earns. What makes him a leader of men and women is how he has learned to interact." (1993, 15) Soft leadership skills can be extraordinarily powerful for any leader. Wilpon's humble approach will earn him a lifetime of loyalty from the people he leads.

This may sound counterintuitive, but allowing yourself to be vulnerable in certain situations can be a strong leadership trait. Sometimes, leaders may not have all the answers; they may need to admit fault for a bad decision, or deliver a tough message such as one about a reduction in the workforce. These are times when leaders must not avoid their teams but face them eye to eye. Don't delegate the reduction in force message to a Human Resource representative—do it yourself. Don't make up an answer to a tough question just to sound like you have it all together; instead be honest and say, "I don't have an answer to that issue right now." Opening yourself up and placing yourself in a vulnerable situation shows you are human, shows you are real, and shows you are member of the same team as everyone else. People respect and appreciate this approach because they realize the leader has nothing to hide. It is a very humble approach to leadership.

William H. Peace concludes his essay with this thought:

Being vulnerable to the give-and-take of ordinary emotional crossfire and intellectual disagreement makes us more human, more credible, and more open to change. (1979, 103)

Who wouldn't enjoy working for this guy?

Be sure to communicate only one message at a time, gather as much input as possible, and don't be afraid to show you're human—and maybe even vulnerable—by opening yourself up to criticism and tough questions. In the end, your team will respect and admire you for your courage.

Stop being ordinary and start thinking how to be an *extraordinary* leader!

Chapter 17

Be Your Best!

"Ability may get you to the top,
but it's character that will keep you there."
—John Wooden

When was the last time you revamped your leadership style?

Tiger Woods, one of the best golfers to ever play the game, is a great example of someone who's the best at his craft, yet has a never-ending thirst to become better. He is constantly tinkering with detail to improve his results. He did so in 2003 by dismantling a golf swing that had led him to eight major championships in just seven years!

If the best player in the world can take an inward look at what's working and what's not, why shouldn't we?

As leaders, this introspective look is critical, and hopefully some of the thoughts in this book will help you in the process. There's always room for improvement, and this is certainly true in the dynamic role of leading people. Our leadership style must evolve and grow with our team, our accomplishments, and our challenges. When you find work that you truly love and have a passion for, the next step becomes doing that work at the highest level of skill, effort, and potential that you can get out of your body and mind.

It really can be viewed in two steps. First, you must love what you do. After you find that, the second step becomes doing that work at the highest level possible to become the best you can. You can only be satisfied and truly fulfilled with results when you know you have given your all. In addition, you will only know what you are capable of when you push yourself to give your best effort.

After just four years in the NFL, the late Sean Taylor who played for the Washington Redskins hit this very epiphany. In September 2007, he told a Fox sports reporter:

> So I just say, I'm healthy right now, I'm going into my fourth year, and why not do the best   that I can? And that's whatever it is, whether it's eating right or training myself right, whether it's studying harder, whatever I can do to better myself. And if you don't take it serious enough, eventually one day you're going to say, Oh, I could have done this, I could have done that.

Wow, Taylor was on his way to understanding the finer points of how to maximize his potential and improve his contributions to his team. But why do some individuals and teams make the leap and others don't?

Jim Collins answered this question and offered a compelling opinion on the development of leadership qualities in his bestseller *Good to Great*. The premise of the book was studying a sampling of firms that grew three times the general stock market return in any fifteen-year period. This produced a small sample of just over twenty companies. Collins then searched for commonalities in how these companies were run. In terms of leadership qualities, he developed a five-level pyramid:

Level 1: Highly Capable Individual—someone who makes solid contributions to the company.

Level 2: Contributing Team Member—an employee who is effective in a team environment.

Level 3: Competent Manager—one who can organize people to achieve results.

Level 4: Effective Leader—one who can rally people around a clear and compelling vision.

Level 5: Executive—builds greatness through a blend of personal humility and professional will.

It's no surprise that all of the companies that went from good to great had level-five leadership within their firms. The definition of a level-five leader may sound simple and be surprising to some; however, it really says it all. **Personal humility** is the ability to show the human side to your team and to understand that the leadership role is just another job that needs to be done. As Darwin E. Smith, ex-CEO of Kimberly-Clark once said, "I never stopped trying to become qualified for the job." Personal humility cannot be defined any better than in that statement. As we discussed earlier, rallying the staff and generating strong followers depends upon these types of soft skills. **Professional will**, on the other hand, is the desire to run the business to the best of your abilities. It is blending your talent and skill with the desire, ambition, and "fire in the belly" to succeed. This type of strength, galvanized with personal humility, is the leadership qualities evidenced by the best companies Collins studied.

However, I believe there is a level-six leader who possesses a trait Collins left out. Level six represents a passionate leader who combines the professional will and personal humility of level five with the ability to bring **creativity and innovation** to the team. An important part of leadership is the ability to think outside the box. People who are creative and innovative are typically inspirational, and people naturally want to follow someone who is inspirational. When you think of some of America's greatest innovators people come to mind such as Henry Ford, Bill Gates, Steve Jobs, Benjamin Franklin, Thomas Jefferson, Walt Disney, Thomas Edison, and the Wright Brothers. Many on this list were great leaders who led their respective companies to be some of America's best.

So, is there a connection between innovators and leaders?

Yes! I believe there are personality traits that are common between innovators and leaders. Innovators need to have creative minds. They are risk takers; they need to sell their ideas to others; they believe in their vision and are driven and focused behind it; they are resilient with a "never say die" attitude. These are all traits we want to see in a good, solid leader. So, my definition of a level-six leader would be a powerful blend of *professional will, personal humility*, and a *creative and innovative spirit.* If creativity and innovation aren't inherent traits for you, just make sure you are sufficiently open-minded to consider all options in a situation and surround yourself with people who *are* innovative. Being an innovator doesn't automatically make for a good leader, but it is a healthy component of leadership, and an important part of the job that can inspire and create strong followers (not to mention new ideas and growth for your team). Innovation and creativity are qualities that will continue to grow and evolve. As a result, leadership styles and leadership strategies will grow and evolve. If we can think it, we can do it and so our work will never be done here.

The title of this chapter, "**Be Your Best**," is really a reminder and a challenge. Delivering your best work takes effort and consistency, along with a plan to chart progress. It also requires the awareness that you need to be your best in front of your team. I once heard the average active person comes into contact with approximately fifty-two people per day. This needs to be viewed as *fifty-two chances* to make a difference, to have an impact, and to inspire.

To test this theory, I would encourage you for one day to keep track of how many people you come into contact with whose interaction you could change their outlook or make their day. I did this on a day I was flying to Phoenix. After just 2 ½ hours from 6 a.m. to 8:30 a.m., I was up to *twelve* people! The people I came into contact with went something like this: my wife, the parking attendant, the shuttle driver, the baggage check attendant, the security line attendant, the person at the gate who took my boarding pass, two stewardesses, the pilot to whom I said good-bye after landing, the Starbucks cashier for my post-flight latte, the baggage claim clerk after my luggage was lost, and a rental car employee.

In just 2 ½ quick hours, I had the ability to leave a positive impression, and to have influence over twelve people. When this example is expanded over fourteen hours in a day, that would total *sixty-seven* people with whom I might have come into contact, so I think fifty-two is probably fairly accurate for many of us. Reflect on your day and think about the people with whom you cross paths. Understand these encounters represent opportunities to have influence, to make a difference, to change thinking, and to actually alter that person's day with your positive attitude. This is how all leaders should think about their daily interactions with their staff, team, or family.

Taking on a leadership role is never easy. It will feel as though you're in a fishbowl with everyone watching your actions and reactions. Your office values and your limits will be tested. Your decisions will be questioned, and the consistency of your logic will be examined. You will see attitudes change as your team experiences good times, but then faces adversity. Your team members will come to you for business problems as well as personal issues.

As a result, it is of paramount importance that you as the leader make fair and consistent decisions because any contradictions will be scrutinized. You must also be genuine with your feelings and advice. Opening yourself up to tough conversations and situations will be healthy because employees respect leaders who "get down in the trenches" with them. If you are a leader with these qualities, trust and respect will naturally follow. Too many times leaders get lazy and want to move straight to motivating their team before building a foundation between themselves and the team members. Make no mistake—you will not get the true potential out of your team until you have established an environment of trust, openness, respect, and excitement. From that point, motivation and inspiration become easy by-products. Then and only then can you realize what your team is capable of, as your *best effort* will now be tangible.

Be your best, lead with passion and make a difference today!

The 8 Steps to Successful Leadership

Learn them, live them, and love them!

(1) Build Your Corral—Establish clear office values and hold *everyone* accountable to them.

(2) Influence—Set direction, align people, and give timely feedback. Include a historical industry perspective in your messaging. *Get your team to see the big picture of what you want to achieve!*

(3) Lead with Enthusiasm and Passion—Employees will model their leader's actions. Set a good example by leading with enthusiasm. It's contagious!

(4) Keep Messages Simple and Focused on Customer—The objective must be simple—to do the best work possible with the least amount of errors on a consistent basis. Make sure the team members from top to bottom are focused on the customer and understand their piece of customer service. Try using storytelling and meaningful quotes to add credibility and depth to your message.

(5) Be Proactive—Being a leader means you need to be at the tip of the sword. A leader beats customers and workers to any potential collisions in the process or service level. A leader who is more reactive than proactive is preparing to fail. As the saying goes, failing to prepare means you are preparing to fail.

(6) Communication—Your success will be defined by how well your staff members execute their work. There is no such thing as over communication. Find creative ways to communicate with your team. Include them on as much as you can because that will encourage them to take ownership of their work. Leadership is a people business!

(7) Be Genuine and Humble—You may even make yourself vulnerable to criticism, but that's OK. Employees respect those who get into the trenches with them.

(8) Be Your Best—Don't become complacent. Take a creative angle in how you lead and how you connect with your staff.

A Leader's Pop Quiz-
10 Questions Every Leader Should Ask

Balance Your Leadership Style by Evaluating the Questions Below

Goals & Expectations Questions

(1) Have I set clear expectations and goals that my team can easily understand and plug into? Are they broken down with weekly, monthly, and annual milestones?

(2) Do I invest in my people? Is there a clear support system when questions arise? Do I proactively offer training?

(3) Have I set up an environment where the entire team focuses on the customer? Have I defined who the customer is?

Communication & Messaging Questions

(4) Are my messages simple and easy to understand? Do I listen and ask questions more than just giving instructions?

(5) Do I acknowledge my team members for a job well done and deliver separate messages of praise versus constructive criticism?

(6) Do I have a consistent way of offering performance feedback? Do I discipline team members in private behind closed doors?

Leader's Growth & Style Questions

(7) Do I make a consistent effort to connect with my team by regularly walking the floor and attending employee celebrations?

(8) *Do I enjoy the work I do?* Do I model a work ethic of trust and mutual respect that I want from my team? If not, find ways to enjoy your work or get out... you can't be a good leader if you're not a good worker.

(9) Do I set aside time to think creatively and be innovative? Do I encourage others to think creatively? Does the team have fun?

(10) Is my leadership style evolving? Am I open to leading in new ways?

Communication Template

On a monthly basis, use the template below to organize your thoughts and deliver a complete message to your team. This template will ensure your message is consistent and complete. The format is simple to follow and easy for your team to digest. You may also invite department heads to offer a guest column so they can highlight an area that deserves special attention from their corner of the company.

Team California Headline News
Our Team News Update – January 2008
Industry News
Current events, stories or news about your industry. Competitor information or changes.
Company News
Current news or announcements from your CEO or corporate office. Company quarterly performance and forecasts.
Team News – Operations & Sales
News pertaining to your office or division. Recent policy or process changes. Show monthly office performance and acknowledge key team members.
Did You Know?
Explain changes to products. Announce new product releases. Bring light to a niche you have over the competition.

—Matt Modugno, 2008

How to Inspire through Storytelling

(Actual weekly e-mails sent to my team)

"If you take care of all the little things, you'll never have a big thing to worry about."
—Cal Ripken, Jr.

Cal Ripken, Jr. was just inducted into the baseball Hall of Fame this past weekend. This quote, however, transcends sports and applies to any walk of life. Why is this quote powerful and something we can learn from?

It speaks to the value of being prepared. It speaks to the power of being organized and having a plan of attack. Lastly, it speaks to having a consistent work ethic and repeating those actions time and time again (Cal's career lasted 20 years and he was known as baseball's "Ironman").

Consistency, Organization, and Preparation ... transfer those skills to your work life today!

"People love to buy, but hate being sold."
—Jeffrey Gitomer

There has been a lot of talk at our branch recently about sales calls that involve things outside of selling. It's called the "No Sales" call.

Why's this a successful sales tactic?

* It fosters a true "connection" with our customers and shows our interest in them is genuine.

* It helps us get to know our customers better outside of the loan they are working on.

* It builds trust and loyalty.

* It may allow you to find a new approach in motivating them to send loans to us.

* It builds a positive "experience" when they think of us … the "customer experience" is a sales tactic of Starbucks and Nordstrom's.

* It avoids the easy way out of product dumping which customers have little time for.

Make our customers feel like they are buying our company, not being sold on our company.

Have a good day.

"You must be active in your own rescue."
—Maritime emergency briefing

For those of you who enjoy cruising the open sea, you will recall this statement being told to you during the emergency briefing as you stood on the main deck and wore a bright orange life vest.

This is one of my favorite quotes because it can be applied to much more than just cruising. It speaks directly at being proactive, responsible, and to have a keen eye as we look ahead and encounter challenges. I have always said that there are two kinds of people in life. One who points their finger outward to other people or circumstances when life is not kind, and the other who is comfortable and confident in pointing their finger inward. People who point their finger inward look for ways to be part of the solution and not the problem. They understand that life's challenges are good for them and enable them to grow as they figure out the solution.

As it relates to any human interaction, those who are thirsty to learn are in deed being active in their own rescue. We must have a strong desire to improve our skills and allow no detour to derail us. As a teacher, one of the greatest gifts you can give your students is the ability to work independently or assimilate in a group to achieve a common goal. Teachers give their students the tools to be active in their own rescue.

Be confident and embrace the finger that's pointed inward so you can improve your contributions as you walk into the future.

"You miss 100 percent of the shots you don't take."
—Wayne Gretzky

Today's market is about taking risks, and more importantly, thinking outside the box. The way we did things in the past may not be the best path for the future. This applies to internal process, policies, and sales approaches as well as having the guts to improve personal skills.

The rules of the game are completely changing before our eyes, and we must be strong and courageous to embrace the future. This is what Gretzky's quote means to me and our branch.

I like what we have going and know everyone is giving 100 percent; however, we can't be lazy or unfocused for a second. It is time to rise up and accept the challenge that is out there every day.

Have a good day.

> *"Forget price—show cost, demonstrate value, list comparisons, prove benefits. If you cannot answer the loan officer in a way that sets you apart from others, you'll never close this (or any) sale."*
> **—Jeffrey Gitomer**

A very powerful and fitting message given today's market. All of us must take the time to craft the way we talk to customers even down to the words we choose. These small details stick in the mind of the customer and will influence them in the future.

The sales managers and I have been working on deliverables to the field that focuses on building value and educating our customer. This has nothing to do with product or price, but will earn us the chance to get future business. We must all think this way and get creative in how we interact with customers.

"Motivation is a fire from within. If someone else tries to light that fire under you, chances are it will burn very briefly."
—Stephen R. Covey

Good reminder from Covey. You can be inspired by someone, but cannot be motivated by someone. True motivation, with long-lasting effects, comes from within you. We talk about the "fire in the belly" and the love for the job … if those are present, it really is amazing what you can achieve. When you think that way, no brick wall is strong enough to hold you back from success … you simply find ways to get through it.

Personal challenges and breakthroughs are great ways to test your internal motivation. If you always wanted to get better at computer skills, if you always wanted to run a marathon or skydive or lose weight … do it! Motivate yourself and do it.

Our very own Harvey Mackay, from the Orange County Register, *writes a weekly column entitled "Lessons in Leadership." His "thoughts of the day" are very powerful.*

Here's a story that is right up our alley …

The wind and the sun were having a conversation one day, which turned into a friendly competition about who was better at making things go their way. The wind said, "I am so strong, and so good at what I do, that I can blow the coat away from that man down on the ground." So the wind blew hard, bending trees and rattling windows. But the stronger the wind, the more the man clutched his coat, wrapping it tight around him.

The sun waited patiently for the windstorm to end, and then took a turn. With a smile, the sun beamed down its warm rays until the man voluntarily took off his coat.

What the wind couldn't do with brutal force, the sun accomplished with warmth and charm. It's a valuable lesson for anyone who has contact with people—now wouldn't that be just about all of us?

When trying to get your way with customers or co-workers, are you the wind or the sun?

Remember, a little charm goes a long way!

The Power of Open-Ended Questions!

Whether you are talking about dating or getting to know your client in mortgage banking, the power of open-ended questions is incredible. It is a way to get other people to talk about themselves, which allow us to learn more about them and their needs. It gives us a clear roadmap on how we can satisfy their needs and build a better relationship.

Here are some open-ended questions that we discussed at our last sales meeting. They are designed to uncover customer needs so we can fulfill those needs.

- ✓ Tell me about your business. What is your strategy? What are you passionate about? What are your business fears? What are your expectations from account reps?
- ✓ Who are you using now, and what do you like about them?
- ✓ Do you agree that diversification is central to the success of most businesses?
- ✓ If you agree, will you allow me the chance to earn your business so you can offer your clients more choices?
- ✓ When you think about our top account reps calling on your office, what service could be improved, or what shortcoming would you like dealt with?

From our friend Jeffrey Gitomer, author of Little Gold Book of YES Attitude:

* Things in life will test your attitude
* Bad service will test your attitude
* Traffic will test your attitude
* Weather will test your attitude
* People will test your attitude
* Arguments will test your attitude
* Life will test your attitude

The secret is: get over it—as fast as you can.

I love this message!

Doing the hard thing is usually the right thing.

Most of society ends up taking the easy or convenient route. Some do this to save time, avoid conflict, or just because they don't want to work at the harder alternative. In life when you're at a crossroads, taking the route that is more difficult is tough because it subjects you to more work or a greater time investment, but I've found in the long run, it is the right decision.

Try it.

Remember, Sales Don't Just Happen …
*80% of sales occur after the **5th call***
*48% of salespeople make one call and **quit***
*24% of salespeople make two calls and **quit***
Only 20% of salespeople keep calling

Persistence is a major part of successful selling. Handling objections and rejection is common, but we must continue to break that wall down to earn business each day! At times it can be draining, but success and winning is very sweet and makes it worth it!

"There is no greater burden than having potential."
—Scott Hamilton

We are fortunate to have a staff filled with overachievers and folks who continue to strive for excellence. Having potential means you are a star employee, and the ongoing challenge is to realize that potential.

I took this quote while watching the ice skating competition at the Olympics last night. The athletes are world class competitors with all of the potential in the world. Their burden is to use this potential and deliver on the greatest stage in the world—the Olympics. Coming home with a medal is the culmination of many hours of practice.

I see this potential in all of you here at Laguna. Our burden is to realize this potential through hard work and commitment as well as experiencing failure but not being derailed by any brick wall we may run into.

Have a great day.

> *"To find true purpose in life, we must find a reward other than something that can be hung on your wall or taken to your bank account."*
>
> —*Fr. Nicholas Dempsey, St. Therese of Carmel*

Maintaining perspective in life at home and at work is one key towards leading a happy life. Focus on the wildly important areas of your life and pour your time and energy there.

Find your purpose and the reward follows!

"My great concern is not whether you have failed but whether you are content with your failure."
—President Abraham Lincoln

Few people failed early in life as much as Lincoln, yet he is regarded as one of our greatest U.S. Presidents.

The message here is to not be afraid to fail, but to learn from it, and to have the determination to improve upon those experiences. We all fail at times; it is the reaction to that failure that is most important in our growth.

"The person who says they can, and the person who says they can't, are both right!"

Which are you?

This message speaks to having determination and a positive outlook and stretching yourself by thinking outside the box!

How do you go from where you are to where you want to be? "Have enthusiasm, a dream, and a goal ... and don't ever give up!"
—Jim Valvano
What does your "Best Effort" look like?

After reviewing our July and seeing some great, positive signs of growth at our office, it's become clear that August can be our best month of 2006 and possibly our best since October 2005! So, the opportunity is there—we just need to grab it.

To get to the finish line it will take a Best Effort from every employee here. We need to have your best performance of the year, and I am not only talking numbers ... service, turn time, solution making ability, attitude, presentations/selling etc. We need our best performance of 2006 right now!

I know we can do it, and it will be fun along the way—I guarantee it!

"Kick your own ass!"

—*Jeffrey Gitomer*

Most of our inspiration and ambition comes from within us, not from others. In his book *The Little Red Book of Sales*, Jeffrey Gitomer talks about the importance of motivating yourself and continually pushing ahead to bigger and better things.

Today, we all need to kick ourselves to learn the nuances of our new rate sheet structure. We will provide training classes and go over examples, but ultimately you must teach yourself and be open-minded to try new ways of understanding how to calculate the interest rate correctly. You must find your comfort zone so that errors are minimized and efficiency is maximized. Motivation and being proactive largely come from within yourself and not from others outside.

Have a good day!

As most of you know by now, I am a big fan of meaningful quotes. I believe we can learn tons from the voices in history. Popular quotes are our only way of getting inside the head of some of our greatest leaders, inventors, athletes, and teachers in U.S. history.

Well, I found one this morning that really hits the nail on the head for me as it relates to our challenges today. Our industry, our company, and we as individuals are all trying to re-invent ourselves for the future. In that spirit, I offer you Mr. Bell's quote:

"When one door closes another door opens; but we so often look so long and so regretfully upon the closed door, that we do not see the ones which open for us."
—Alexander Graham Bell

Opportunities are always present. It just takes the right frame of mind, the right proactive work ethic, and a positive attitude to make it happen.

Have a good day.

Is the glass half empty or half full?

There is power in your answer to this question because it can change how you approach life, which in turn has major trickle-down effects like:

1- Whether you are successful or not.
2- Whether you find happiness or not.
3- People like to be around positive people so this may determine your quality of friends.
4- Helps your ability to get through tough times or struggles.
5- When you have a positive outlook, things tend to fall into place more easily.

While I was researching the genesis of this very commonly used phrase, I found that people have formed meeting groups and societies around this cause. It is amazing how this very simple teaching has impacted many people around the world!

Think about it and apply it today because we all know we are faced with this choice in today's marketplace!

My take is this: the glass is twice the size it needs to be, so it is full! :)

Perspective is a wonderful thing. Everyone must keep a grounded and realistic perspective. It is the easiest thing to lose sight of but keeps our expectations in line and maintains our humility through life.

Educator Charles Sykes, author of 50 Rules Kids Won't Learn in School, *reminds us of some great points to remember and things to keep in perspective.*

Rule 1: Life is not fair—get used to it!

Rule 2: The world won't care about your self-esteem. The world will expect you to accomplish something *before* you feel good about yourself.

Rule 3: You will NOT make $60,000 a year right out of high school. You won't be a vice-president with a car phone until you earn both.

Rule 4: If you think your teacher is tough, wait till you get a boss.

Rule 5: Flipping burgers is not beneath your dignity. Your grandparents had a different word for burger flipping: they called it opportunity.

Rule 6: If you mess up, it's not your parents' fault, so don't whine about your mistakes, learn from them.

Rule 7: Before you were born, your parents weren't as boring as they are now. They got that way from paying your bills, cleaning your clothes, and listening to you talk about how cool you thought you were.

So before you save the rain forest from the parasites of your parents' generation, try delousing (getting rid of lice) the closet in your own room.

Rule 8: Your school may have done away with winners and losers, but life **has not**. In some schools, they have abolished failing grades and they'll give you as *many times* as you want to get the right answer. This doesn't bear the slightest resemblance to **anything** in real life.

Rule 9: Life is not divided into semesters. You don't get summers off, and very few employers are interested in helping you *find yourself*. Do that on your own time.

Rule 10: Television is *not* real life. In real life people actually have to leave the coffee shop and go to jobs.

Rule 11: Be nice to nerds. Chances are you'll end up working for one.

This sign hangs in our lobby for employees to be reminded of the effort level expected of them and for customers to see our dedication level to them.

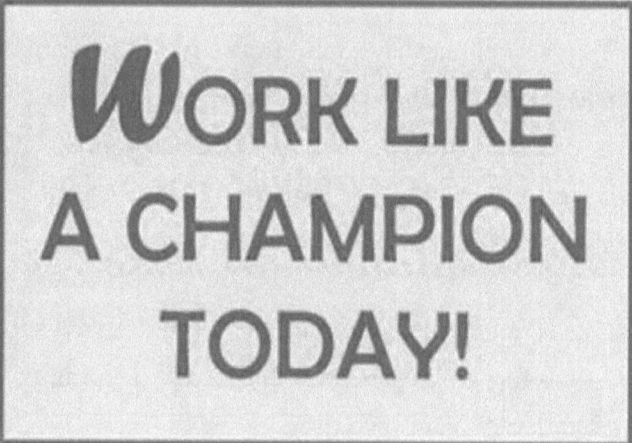

Every day we have the choice to make it a great day or a terrible one. We control our attitude every day. We may be tired, frustrated, or have just argued with our spouse or roommate; however, when we walk through the front doors at work, this sign will serve as a reminder of the effort level expected. We will not be a regular office; we will be a Champion office!

A major league baseball player fails seven out of ten times and is considered an All Star. That person might even make the Hall of Fame!

Failure at the plate is a huge part of the game of baseball. It is how one deals with failure that makes the difference between an All Star player and the underachiever.

The same is true in the business world or in life in general. We must use failure as learning experiences to make us better. If we allow failure to drag us down or feel victimized, we will not grow from the experience. True growth is achieved when we allow ourselves to get to the edge of our comfort zone and understand that failure may result. Persistence and learning from our failure is the key to growth.

"I am a success because I have failed more times than anyone in history."

—Michael Jordan

Build Your Own Narratives with Business-Relevant Quotes

Topics:

Attitude
Work Ethic
Proactivity
Perspective

Attitude

"We either make ourselves miserable or we make ourselves strong. The amount of work is the same."
　　—Carlos Castaneda

"The pessimist sees difficulty in every opportunity. The optimist sees the opportunity in every difficulty."
　　—Winston Churchill

"It's always the right time to do the right thing."
　　—Martin Luther King, Jr.

"You can accomplish anything in life, provided that you do not mind who gets the credit."
　　—Harry S. Truman

"Humility is not thinking less of yourself, it's thinking of yourself less."
　　—Rick Warren

"When you believe you can – you can!"
　　—Maxwell Maltz

"Play Like a Champion Today."
　　—Notre Dame Football (locker room message)

"We should not let our fears hold us back from pursuing our hopes."
—John F. Kennedy

"The mind is the limit. As long as the mind can envision the fact that you can do something, you can do it – as long as you really believe a 100 percent."
—Arnold Schwarzenegger

"The greatest discovery of my generation is that human beings can alter their lives by altering their attitudes of mind."
—William James

"You miss 100 percent of the shots you don't take."
—Wayne Gretzky

"The most important single ingredient in the formula of success is knowing how to get along with people."
—Theodore Roosevelt

"The one without dreams is the one without wings."
—Muhammad Ali

"Your chances of success in any undertaking can always be measured by your belief in yourself."
—Robert Collier

"Pessimism is an excuse for not trying and a guarantee to a personal failure."
—Bill Clinton

"People of mediocre ability sometimes achieve outstanding success because they don't know when to quit. Most people succeed because they are determined to."
—George E. Allen

"You must be the change that you want to see in the world."
—Mahatma Ghandi

"With confidence, you have won even before you have started."
—Marcus Garvey

"If it can be done, we can do it...that's all there is to it!"
—Unknown

"Too many of us are not living our dreams because we are living our fears."
—Les Brown

"Progress occurs when courageous, skillful leaders seize the opportunity to change things for the better."
—Harry S. Truman

"Here's what you need to understand about life. There are going to be things that happen to you that you have no control over. So why spend time being upset over things you have no damn control over? Spend time doing the things you want to and enjoy versus the things that are happening to you."
—Bob Knight

"Do not go where the path may lead, go where there is no path and leave a trail."
—Ralph Waldo Emerson

"Whether you think you can or think you can't, you are right."
—Henry Ford

"Whoever is happy will make others happy too."
—Anne Frank

"Nothing great was ever achieved without enthusiasm."
—Ralph Waldo Emerson

"People with integrity do what they say they are going to do. Others have excuses."
 —Unknown

"Creativity takes courage."
 —Unknown

"It is always fun to do the impossible."
 —Walt Disney

"It takes a strong person to stand up for themselves. It takes a stronger person to stand up for others."
 —Unknown

"The way we communicate with others and with ourselves ultimately determines the quality of our lives."
 —Anthony Robbins

"Mental toughness is what wins championships. You must respect everyone and fear nothing."
 —Ben Howland, UCLA basketball coach

"The task ahead is never as great as the strength inside."
 —Unknown

"My life started to become great when I stopped asking 'why me?'"

  —Darryl Stingley, New England Patriots wide receiver who became a quadriplegic

"Enthusiasm is the electricity of life. How do you get it? You act enthusiastic until you make it a habit."

  —Gordon Parks

"You can do anything if you have enthusiasm. Enthusiasm is the yeast that makes your hopes rise to the stars. With it, there is accomplishment. Without it there are only alibis."

  —Henry Ford

"I studied the lives of great men and women, and I found that the men and women who got to the top were those who did the jobs they had in hand, with everything they had of energy and enthusiasm."

  —Henry Ford

"We play for the name on the front of the jersey, not the one on the back of it."

  —Tommy Lasorda

"If we worked on the assumption that what is accepted as true really is true, then there would be little hope for advance."
—Orville Wright

"If birds can glide for long periods of time, then…why can't I?"
—Orville Wright

"We could hardly wait to get up in the morning."
—Wilbur Wright

"I have not failed. I've just found 10,000 ways that won't work."
—Thomas A. Edison

"Life is 10% what happens to me and 90% of how I react to it."
—Charles R. Swindoll

"Winners simply do the things losers won't."
—Unknown

"We know you have a choice where you send your business, so we appreciate you chose us."
　　　—Southwest Airlines marketing slogan

"You can always become better. People ask me, 'Are you there yet?' I say 'No.' You never get there. And that's the great thing about it. You can always be better the next day. That's how I look at golf and how I look at life. You can always be better."
　　　—Tiger Woods

"Most things I worry about never happen anyway."
　　　—Tom Petty

"Anyone who has never made a mistake has never tried anything new."
　　　—Albert Einstein

"Always be humble, always be kind, always be respectful, and always compete."
　　　—Pete Carroll

"Confidence shared is better than confidence only in yourself."
　　　—Mike Krzyzewski

"Honesty is the best policy."
   —Benjamin Franklin

"Conformity is the jailer of freedom and the enemy of growth."
   —John F. Kennedy

"If you can dream it, you can do it."
   —Walt Disney

"Are you afraid to lose or determined to win? Which one are you?"
   —NCAA Tournament, March Madness

"How do you go from where you are to where you want to be? Have enthusiasm, a dream, and a goal ... and don't ever give up!"
   —Jim Valvano

Work Ethic

"If a guy gives you 5 bucks, you give him 7 bucks worth of work."
　　　—Bill Russell

"I'm a great believer in luck, and I find the *harder I work*, the more I have of it."
　　　—Thomas Jefferson

"If you work hard, good things will come."
　　　—Charles Gwynn (told to Tony Gwynn, his son)

"Excellence is the gradual result of always striving to do better."
　　　—Pat Riley

"Look after the customer and the business will take care of itself."
　　　—Ray Kroc

"Three great essentials to achieve anything worthwhile are, first, hard work; second, stick-to-itiveness; third, common sense."
　　　—Thomas Edison

"I don't know if I practiced more than anyone, but I practiced enough. If someone was practicing more than me, it would bother me."
—Larry Bird

"I never stopped trying to become qualified for the job."
—Darwin Smith

"The harder you work, the harder it is to surrender."
—Vince Lombardi

"I am a success because I have failed more times than anyone in history."
—Michael Jordan

"There is no greater burden than having potential."
—Scott Hamilton

"There's never a traffic jam on the extra mile, not many people travel that far."
—Harvey McKay

"As we express our gratitude, we must never forget that the highest appreciation is not to utter words, but to live by them."
—John F. Kennedy

"You never know what twist will pop that can open."
—Tim Russert

"If you live long enough, you'll make mistakes. But if you learn from them, you'll be a better person. It's how you handle adversity, not how it affects you. The main thing is never quit, never quit, never quit."
—Bill Clinton

"When you are up against your biggest challenge, you define yourself."
—LaDanian Tomlinson

"Teams rarely succeed unless they have fun in what they are doing."
—Dale Carnegie

"Any fool can criticize, condemn and complain and most fools do."
—Benjamin Franklin

"You're going to fall on your face, you're going to learn from it, and you're going to continue that for the rest of your life."
—Warren Bennis

"The difference between the impossible and the possible lies in a person's determination."
　　—Tommy Lasorda

"You've got to get up every morning with determination if you're going to go to bed with satisfaction."
　　—George Lorimer

"There is a place in the world for anyone who says, 'I'll take care of it.'"
　　—Unknown

"Early to bed, early to rise, work like hell and advertise!"
　　—Ted Turner

"Humility and class never go out of style."
　　—Matt Modugno

"How committed are you? There is a remarkable difference between 99% and 100%."
　　—Vic Conant

"He that is good for making excuses is seldom good for anything else."
　　—Benjamin Franklin

"I do not like to repeat successes, I like to go on to other things."
　　　—Walt Disney

"If you want to be the best, you've got to beat the best."
　　　—Unknown

"Know your strengths, but know your weaknesses better."
　　　—Warren Bennis

"When people believe in something very deeply, things happen."
　　　—Cesar Chavez

"As we express our gratitude, we must never forget that the highest appreciation is not to utter words, but to live by them."
　　　—John F. Kennedy

"If you do what you've always done, you'll get what you've always gotten."
　　　—Anthony Robbins

"Leadership is practiced not so much in words as in attitude and in actions."
　　　—Unknown

"The only way to get the best out of it, is to put your best into it."
　　　—Snoop Dogg

"An investment in knowledge pays the best interest."
　　　—Benjamin Franklin

"Success is a journey, not a destination."
　　　—Bill Russell

"Excellence is not a singular act, but a habit. We are what we repeatedly do."
　　　—Aristotle

"The greater the difficulty, the more glory in surmounting it."
　　　—Epictetus

"Winners never quit and quitters never win."
　　　—Vince Lombardi

"If you can help people solve their problems, the world is your oyster."
　　　—Dale Carnegie

"There is always a place in the world (or on the team) for anyone who says, 'I'll take care of it.'"
　　　—Harvey McKay

"Change happens from the bottom up, not the top down."
 —Barack Obama

"There are no shortcuts to any place worth going."
 —Beverly Sills

"You must be active in your own rescue."
 —Maritime emergency briefing to passengers.

"The way to get started is to quit talking and begin doing."
 —Walt Disney

Proactivity

"The only way to stay on top is to keep getting better."
    —Tiger Woods

"Inspect what you expect."
    —Franklin Covey

"If you take care of all the little things, you'll never have a big thing to worry about."
    —Cal Ripken, Jr.

"There is no substitute for preparation, work ethic, and organization."
    —Unknown

"Always do your best. What you plant now, you will harvest later."
    —Unknown

"The ability to concentrate and to use your time well is everything if you want to succeed in business--or almost anywhere else for that matter."
    —Lee Iacocca

"If you don't know where you are going, you'll end up some place else."
—Yogi Berra

"Even if you're on the right track, you'll get run over if you just sit there."
—Will Rogers

"I believe in being an innovator."
—Walt Disney

"By failing to prepare, you are preparing to fail."
—Benjamin Franklin

"The future has a way of arriving unannounced."
—George Will

"Begin with the end in mind."
—Stephen Covey

"Life is not about waiting for the storm to pass -- it's about learning how to dance in the rain."
—Unknown

Perspective

"Just when everyone is saying how great you are is when you're the most vulnerable."
—Walt Disney

"Imagination is more important than knowledge."
—Albert Einstein

"Nothing is particularly hard if you divide it into small jobs."
—Henry Ford

"To find purpose in life, we must find a reward other than something that can be hung on your wall or deposited into your bank account."
—Fr. Nicholas Dempsey, Pastor, Saint Therese of Carmel

"I am not concerned with the return *on* my money, as much as the return *of* my money."
—Will Rogers

"It takes 20 years to build a reputation and five minutes to ruin it. If you think about that, you'll do things differently."
　　—Warren Buffett

"If you want the rainbow, you've got to put up with the rain."
　　—Jimmy Durante

"Pain is temporary. Quitting lasts forever."
　　—Lance Armstrong

"The ultimate measure of man is not where he stands in moments of comfort and convenience, but where he stands at times of challenge and controversy."
　　—Martin Luther King, Jr.

"When you change the way you look at things, the things you look at change."
　　—Wayne Dyer

"Adversity. I would never have amounted to anything had I not been forced to come up the hard way."
　　—J.C. Penney

"We cannot build our own future without helping others to build theirs."
　　—Bill Clinton

"Money doesn't change men, it merely unmasks them. If a man is naturally selfish or arrogant or greedy, the money brings that out, that's all."
　　—Henry Ford

"A life is not important except in the impact it has on other lives."
　　—Jackie Robinson

"A man wrapped up in himself makes a very small bundle."
　　—Benjamin Franklin

"If you think pennies you'll make pennies. If you think dollars you'll make dollars."
　　—Unknown

"We have 2 ears and 1 mouth because listening is twice as important as speaking."
　　—Unknown

"To succeed … you need to find something to hold on to, something to motivate you, something to inspire you."
　　—Tony Dorsett

"Winning a basketball game does not mean more to me than helping people."
　　—Mike Krzyzewski

"You will discover new oceans when you allow yourself to lose sight of the shore."
    —Unknown

"Ability may get you to the top, but it's character that will keep you there."
    —John Wooden

"Winners are those people who make a habit of doing the things losers are uncomfortable doing."
    —Unknown

"The cost of victory is high—but so are the rewards."
    —Paul "Bear" Bryant

"Do what you can, with what you have, where you are."
    —Theodore Roosevelt

"Things turn out best for the people who make the best of the way things turn out."
    —John Wooden

"At twenty years of age the will reigns; at thirty, the wit; and at forty, the judgment."
    —Benjamin Franklin

"When one door closes another door opens; but we so often look so long and so regretfully upon the closed door, that we do not see the ones which open for us."
   —Alexander Graham Bell

"All the adversity I've had in my life, all my troubles and obstacles, have strengthened me ... You may not realize it when it happens, but a kick in the teeth may be the best thing in the world for you."
   —Walt Disney

"Courage is resistance to fear; mastery of fear—not absence of fear."
   —Mark Twain

"Motivation is a fire from within. If someone else tries to light that fire under you, chances are it will burn very briefly."
   —Stephen R. Covey

"Leave the world a better place than you found it."
   —Unknown

"Forget price—show cost, demonstrate value, list comparisons, prove benefits. If you cannot answer the customer in a way that sets you apart from others, you'll never close any sale."
   —Jeffrey Gitomer

"Focus on what you can control, and don't derail yourself with those things you cannot."
—Lance Armstrong

"Without struggle there is no purpose."
—Unknown

"Growth happens when you put yourself on the edge of your comfort zone."
—Unknown

"Genuine leadership comes from the quality of your vision and your ability to spark others to extraordinary performance."
—Jack Welch

"It is possible to fly without motors, but not without knowledge and skill."
—Wilbur Wright

"Opportunity is missed by most people because it is dressed in overalls and looks like work."
—Thomas A. Edison

"Change has a considerable psychological impact on the human mind. To the fearful it is threatening because it means that things may get worse. To the hopeful it is encouraging because things may get better. To the

confident it is inspiring because the challenge exists to make things better."
—King Whitney, Jr.

"Golf is definitely cool now. It wasn't when I was a kid, but I kept doing it because I loved it."
—Tiger Woods

"You are never strong enough that you don't need help."
—Cesar Chavez

"No matter what you've done for yourself or for humanity, if you can't look back on having given love and attention to your own family, what have you really accomplished?"
—Lee Iacocca

"My dad always taught me these words: care and share. That's why we put on clinics. The only thing I can do is try to give back. If it works, it works."
—Tiger Woods

"Doing the hard thing is usually the right thing."
—Unknown

"Luck is where preparatin meets opportunity."
—Unknown

"When I was a boy of fourteen, my father was so ignorant I could hardly stand to have the old man around. But when I got to be twenty-one, I was astonished at how much he had learned in seven years."
—Mark Twain, 1874

"Always be humble, always be kind, always be respectful, and always compete."
—Pete Carroll

"Life is only as complicated as we make it."
—Matt Modugno

"A calm sea does not make a skillful mariner."
—Unknown

"I only hope that we don't lose sight of one thing – that is was all started by a mouse."
—Walt Disney

"Character is higher than intellect."
—Ralph Waldo Emerson

"Honesty is the first chapter in the book of wisdom."
—Thomas Jefferson

"You know you're getting old when all you talk about is what you've done and not what you are going to do."
—Bill Russell

"Seek first to understand, then to be understood."
—Stephen Covey

"Efforts and courage are not enough without purpose and direction."
—John F. Kennedy

"To lead is to serve."
—Bill Russell

"When times become hard, the best become better and the worst disappear."
—Max Azria

"Experience is what you get when you don't get what you want."
—Randy Pausch

"When you enjoy the journey, everything else is downhill."
—Clyde Drexler

"Good leadership is a lifestyle that we must practice everyday."
—Matt Modugno

... and for proof that great leaders can have a great sense of humor ...

"Beer is living proof that God loves us and wants us to be happy."
  —Benjamin Franklin

"In my position, I don't think about me, I think about the players."
  —Bud Black

"Our actions and our words should coincide."
  —Father Nicholas Dempsey

"Disneyland will never be completed. It will continue to grow as long as there is imagination left in the world."
  —Walt Disney

"You just have to do good, and you have to think well, and you have to be concerned about people who have less than you have. I guess I do have more credits than debits in my life."
  —Paul Newman

Why the 2007 Mortgage Meltdown Happened

*"But how do we know when **irrational exuberance** has unduly escalated asset values, which then become subject to unexpected and prolonged contractions."*
- Alan Greenspan, December 1996

The business landscape on which my team and I performed was the financial services industry, more specifically as a lender of home loans. We offered first and second mortgages in both purchase and refinance scenarios. Historically, the mortgage business is actually a very conservative business. Traditionally, home loans require equity or a down payment with the loan being backed by the asset such as a single family residence or condo. Usually the rate is fixed, or on an adjustable rate mortgage the payment increases are reasonable and predictable. So, the investor who buys and services home loans is insulated from risk in a couple of different ways. First, the investor has rights to the property if the borrower defaults on the loan, and second, the investor has built-in equity via the down payment to assist in the cost of selling or renting the property.

The mortgage business is a great industry where one can truly help a borrower in need to reduce monthly payments or take cash out for college tuition, or to lend a helping hand to someone with life events such as divorce, death of a family member, or illness. The joy of closing a loan that truly benefits and changes a borrower's life is a feeling like no other. However, like any product or service that gets into the hands of the wrong people, the mortgage business also has a dark side where borrowers are taken advantage by exorbitant loan fees, loan terms that are not fully understood by the borrower, or pure greed. In early 2007, this historically conservative industry became one of the most lethal and dangerous in America. *Why?*

In 2007, news of the mortgage industry became the center of attention. The term *subprime* went from obscurity to a household buzzword. It gained so much popularity in our culture that the American Dialect Society voted *subprime* the 2007 Word of the Year over such contenders as *green* and *Googleganger*. However, those who understood the events unfolding realized the danger subprime loans represented. In a January 2008 press release, Wayne Glowka, a spokesman for the American Dialect Society and a dean at Reinhardt College in Waleska, GA, said, "It's affecting all kinds of people in all kinds of places."

A similar "boom and bust" episode can be seen in the technology industry of the late 1990s. Tech companies were innovative and successful, and it seemed as if nothing could stop the momentum the Silicon Valley was experiencing. Finding venture capital for tech startup companies was easy because investors hoped to create the next Hewlett-Packard or Apple. Gradually, stock market players and investors ventured further and further from the core fundamentals of the way to analyze a company for investment purposes because the upside seemed such a sure thing. Even when price-to-earnings ratios became laughable, money kept pouring into this sector.

In the late 1990s, then-Federal Reserve Chairman Alan Greenspan tried to warn the public by describing what was happening in the tech sector using the words *irrational exuberance*. I call it blind optimism. Either way, the descriptions reflected a situation that was dangerous for consumers because when a market is in this "red hot" state, it's usually not based on solid fundamentals and will likely falter.

Fast forward to the last few months of 2001. A very similar situation was revealed in the housing and finance sector after the 9/11 tragedy. Not only will 2001 be remembered for what happened that day, but the year will be emblematic of when Greenspan and the Federal Reserve began to take serious notice of a faltering economy and tried to spark growth. To avoid a recession, the Fed approved thirteen consecutive rate deceases from January

2001 to June 2003. Over this period, the Federal Funds Rate went from 6.25 percent to 1 percent and moved mortgage interest rates to their lowest levels in over forty years! The "Perfect Storm" when financing was ripe for both purchase and refinance transactions was upon us. By the end of 2001 and beginning of 2002, the housing, real estate, and finance sectors were beginning to sprint.

Just like a human body's basic organs are a heart, liver and kidney, the basic components of a home loan are a *credit report, income history*, and *property valuation*. Those three areas that serve as the heartbeat of any home loan are essential for an underwriter to review regarding loan approval. So, if you want to make it easier for borrowers to qualify for loans, the lender simply adjusts what it expects from these three levers. As long as an investor is willing to buy and service the loan based on those qualifying parameters, a lender can build a business model and the lending machine continues to operate.

From 2001 to 2005, home price appreciation (HPA) was growing at a rapid pace fueled by low interest rates and a very robust housing sector. As long as prices were growing, the loans being written performed well and appeared very stable. Why would borrowers default on their loan when their home was appreciating in value every month?

With a solid housing industry and loans that were paying on time, qualifying guidelines began to be stretched. Wall Street investors purchasing home loans were interested in taking on more risk because the ground seemed very stable. The ordinary loan was OK, but a little more risk might mean a greater yield in return. Just like Evel Knievel who with each successful jump needed to add one more car to satisfy his appetite for risk, the mortgage industry was expanding loan qualifying guidelines beyond what was prudent. This was evident when looking at the evolution of what would later be called "boutique" or "exotic" financing.

In the mid-1990s, we saw the first mainstream 100 percent financing loan surface in subprime lending. This was comprised of an 80 percent first mortgage and a 20 percent second mortgage with no down payment required. This loan did require a two-year history of income evidenced by pay stubs and W2s, which is what the industry calls full income documentation. However, by the late 1990s, twelve months of bank statements were acceptable as income documentation. This opened the door to fraud and made lenders vulnerable to it as it was more difficult to validate bank statements than pay stubs or W2s.

By 2000, the industry saw guidelines becoming even more aggressive to allow a 55 percent debt-to-income ratio. This meant that 55 percent of the borrowers' *gross income* could be used to service all of their obligations between their home, credit cards, and installment debt. To give some perspective, historically the industry would frown on a borrower who had a debt ratio above 40 percent. Now, the industry was approving borrowers for 100 percent financing who were 55 percent encumbered in debt.

At about this same time, the industry introduced the interest-only loan. Here the monthly payment would only pay the interest on the loan without gradually reducing the principal owed. This was the equivalent of a borrower running in place and making no progress in paying down the loan.

Then around 2003, we saw loan programs become their most aggressive in an attempt to keep a hot housing market alive. Lenders began offering 100 percent financing on programs that asked for absolutely *no* income documentation. This was known as a stated 100 percent loan. So, the 100 percent program went from requiring pay stubs and W2s to only bank statements, then to nothing!

Finally in 2003, one of the most toxic loans hit the market: the payment option loan. This allowed a borrower to choose from four monthly payments with the lowest and most appealing one incurring negative amortization to the loan balance. This program actually allowed a loan balance to grow beyond what a home was worth because the monthly payment did not cover the interest owed. The most horrific aspect here is that lending guidelines allowed all of these loan features to be present simultaneously. The degree of difficulty for borrower repayment was at the highest point it could be.

In the underwriting of loans, there is what's called *layered risk*. This term is used when one loan has multiple factors that represent risk to the borrower and lender. It is a common reason a loan application will be declined. An example of a loan with layered risk might be a borrower who had sporadic credit late payments coupled with a recent change of jobs to work in a new industry where the person had no previous experience. In addition, let's assume the appraiser struggled to find worthy comparables to justify the appraised value. So in essence we have one problem in each of the major areas of a loan: a credit issue, income problem, and property concern. Any one issue by itself might be resolved, but all three together create a high risk situation. An underwriter would evaluate the degree of risk, identify any offsetting positive factors, and render a decision.

This is an example of layered risk from a borrower qualifying perspective, and guidelines were constructed to monitor and control these situations. However, between the product risk mentioned above and the layered risk from a borrower profile, the degree of overall loan risk could be great. Let's review how the product evolution we summarized above could make for a toxic loan that has little to no chance to succeed.

Subprime Loan Features and Layered Risk

Toxic Feature	Why It's a Risk
12 months' bank statements or stated income	Not a true picture of a borrower's earnings.
100% financing, no down payment required	No immediate equity.
Interest-only payments	Short-term solution, payment will rise.
55% debt to income ratio	Stretches borrower's capacity to repay debt.
Payment options including negative amortization	Equity eater. Allows loan amount to grow larger than value of home.
Short- term adjustable loans (i.e., 1-year or 2-year fixed) with high margins	High margins drive monthly payment much higher once fixed period ends. Borrower affordability becomes a major concern as loan qualification was based only on initial payment.

The column on the left above reads like a home loan flyer from the early 2000s as to what was advertised and available. The column on the right above represents all the potential pitfalls which were realized starting in 2006 with what would be labeled the "subprime meltdown." As the housing market weakened and home price appreciation (HPA) came to a halt, borrowers had yet another major concern with their equity position. Now it wasn't just the loan program that was working against them—the market was as well. The combination of these two factors accelerated the meltdown as borrowers had a very bleak home balance sheet.

Who's to blame?

Well, there are many opinions flying around and fingers being pointed. One thing is for sure: the mortgage industry will undergo revolutionary change to ensure better lending fundamentals are applied to the risks mentioned above. In terms of blame, I believe it is shared across the industry, up through Wall Street, through the regulatory offices, and down to the borrower level. Wall Street bought the loans and allowed the machine to continue operating, regulatory offices were asleep at the wheel and did not try to proactively keep a finger on the pulse of the industry, lenders expanded guidelines beyond reasonable levels, loan officers did not always educate their borrowers of the potential pitfalls and raise awareness to future payment increases, and some borrowers were greedy and bought above their means, stretching themselves beyond healthy limits. Thus, the responsibility was shared.

During the dot-com bust in the late 1990s, P/E ratios were out of whack with technology businesses being built solely on an idea and a hope with no established earnings. In the early 2000s, the housing boom fueled by historically low interest rates created a large snowball effect as home values continued to rise to very lofty levels. In both examples, the degree of risk was large, and both sectors ventured far from the basic fundamentals and core strategies required to run solid businesses.

So, the "irrational exuberance" in the marketplace that occurred twice in the eight years between 2000 and 2007 left many casualties. The mortgage meltdown represented the challenge I needed to face as a leader.

Regardless of the type of adversity you may confront, it becomes the responsibility of you as the leader to guide, communicate, and find ways to maintain a positive and constructive path for you and your team. Anyone can lead during thriving times, but it is in adverse times that you discover what you and your team are made of.

Bennis, Warren G. "Interview with Warren Bennis by
   David E. Wright." In *Conversations on Leadership*.
   Sevierville, TN: Insight, 2004

Bennis, Warren G. "Where Have All the Leaders Gone?"

In *Contemporary Issues in Leadership*, edited by William E.

Rosenbach & Robert L. Taylor. 2nd edition. Boulder, CO:
   Westview Press, 1989.

Blanchard, Kenneth, and Norman Vincent Peale. *The
   Power of Ethical Management*. New York: William
   Morrow, 1988.

Carnegie, Dale. *The Leader In You*. New York: Pocket
   Books, 1993.

Chandler, Steve. *Reinventing Yourself*. Franklin Lakes, NJ:
   The Career Press, 2005.

Collins, Jim. *Good To Great: Why Some Companies Make
   the Leap … and Others Don't*. New York: Harper
   Collins, 2001.

Covey, Stephen R. *The Four Disciplines of Execution*. Salt Lake City, UT: Franklin Covey, 2004.

Cronin, Thomas E. "Thinking and Learning About Leadership." In *Contemporary Issues in Leadership*, edited by William E. Rosenbach & Robert L. Taylor. 2nd edition. Boulder, CO: Westview Press, 1989.

Crother, Cyndi, and the crew of World Famous Pike Place Fish Market. *Catch! A Fishmonger's Guide to Greatness*. San Francisco: Berrett-Koehler, 2004.

Ehmann, Lain Chroust. "Flex Your Power: How to Develop the Will and Skill to be a Leader" (2007). *Selling Power*. November/December 2007, Volume 27, Number 9: 64.

Fulmer, Phillip. "Interview with Phillip Fulmer by David E. Wright." In *Conversations on Leadership*. Sevierville, TN: Insight, 2004.

Genovese, Michael A. *Memo to a New President: The Art and Science of Presidential Leadership*. New York: Oxford University Press, 2008.

Gilliland, Steve. "Interview with Steve Gilliland by David E. Wright" (2004). In *Conversations On Leadership*. Sevierville, Tennessee: Insight Publishing Company.

Gitomer, Jeffrey. *Little Gold Book of YES! Attitude.* New Jersey: Prentice Hall, 2006.

Gitomer, Jeffrey. *The Little Red Book of Selling.* Austin, Texas: Bard Press, 2005.

Goffee, Robert, and Gareth Jones. "Followership: It's Personal, Too" (1979), *Harvard Business Review on Breakthrough Leadership.* Boston, MA: Harvard Business School Publishing Corporation.

Isbouts, Jean-Pierre. *Discovering Walt: The Magical Life of Walt Disney.* New York: A Roundtable Press Book, 2001.

Lencioni, Patrick. *Death by Meeting: A Leadership Fable about Solving the Most Painful Problem in Business.* San Francisco: Jossey-Bass, 2004.

Peace, William H. "The Hard Work of Being a Soft Manager" *Harvard Business Review on Breakthrough Leadership.* Boston, MA: Harvard Business School, 1979.

Sanborn, Mark. *The Fred Factor.* New York: Doubleday, 2004.

Sykes, Charles J. *50 Rules Kids Won't Learn in School.* New York: St. Martin's Press, 2007.

Matt Modugno is a leadership consultant and founder of Sago Capital Management. He spent 18 years in the financial services industry and held a variety of leadership positions. His office earned several company records for production, turn-time, and customer satisfaction.

Matt studied Political Science and earned his degree from Loyola Marymount University. He lives in San Diego, CA with his wife, Stacy, and his two children, Samantha and Luke.

Matt Modugno can be reached at mattsleadership@yahoo.com